FACING THE GREEN BAY PACKERS

PLAYERS RECALL THE GLORY YEARS OF THE TEAM FROM TITLETOWN USA

EDITED BY CHUCK CARLSON

Foreword by Ron Wolf

SPORTS PUBLISHING

Sports Publishing books may be purchased in bulk at special discounts for sales promotion, corporate gifts, fund-raising, or educational purposes. Special editions can also be created to specifications. For details, contact the Special Sales Department, Sports Publishing, 307 West 36th Street, 11th Floor, New York, NY 10018 or sportspubbooks@skyhorsepublishing.com.

Sports Publishing® is a registered trademark of Skyhorse Publishing, Inc.®, a Delaware corporation.

Visit our website at www.sportspubbooks.com.

10 9 8 7 6 5 4 3 2 1

Library of Congress Cataloging-in-Publication Data is available on file.

Cover design by Tom Lau
Cover photo credit AP

ISBN: 978-1-61321-929-4
Ebook ISBN: 978-1-61321-930-0

Printed in the United States of America

CONTENTS

FOREWORD

By Ron Wolf

IN NOVEMBER 1991 Bob Harlan, the Green Bay Packers chief executive officer, offered me what I considered to be the opportunity of a lifetime. He was looking for a new general manager to help change the culture and direction of a franchise that had not accomplished a great deal for the better part of the previous twenty-eight years.

Bob told me it would not be an easy job. However, he also promised I'd have all the resources necessary to help me carve out a new path. I wanted to prove that after twenty-eight years in the player personnel departments of the Oakland/Los Angeles Raiders and the New York Jets (I was the de facto general manager of the Tampa Bay Buccaneers at the start of that franchise), I could run a franchise. Many of my friends in pro football told me to turn the job down. They saw Green Bay as a football wasteland. They knew that players from other organizations viewed the Packers as the last stop in their football lives, literally an exile, if you will, to the frozen tundra, with no hope of success.

The Packers had not won a world championship since 1968, when they beat the team I worked for at that time, the Oakland Raiders. Since then, the Packers had reached the playoffs only twice (one of those a strike year) and had won just one playoff game.

I admit I did not know any of this when Bob and I first talked about my taking over the general manager role. It wasn't until the late great Packers public relations director Lee Remmel, who knew more about Packers history than anyone ever will, explained to me the remarkable history of this magnificent franchise that I understood the enormity of the position I had been handed.

And what a wonderful experience it became.

I recall the local media reported when I was hired that I would get the kind of power not seen by a Green Bay Packers executive since the days of Vince Lombardi. That was a lot to absorb. After all, to be mentioned in the same sentence with the Green Bay Packers and Vince Lombardi was an honor unto itself.

We got the job done. We found a franchise quarterback in Brett Favre, a head coach in Mike Holmgren, we brought in a lot of other great players, and with our scouting staff we assembled a team that would not only be competitive, but would win one Super Bowl, go to another, and re-establish the Packers as a powerful, proud franchise our fans deserved.

As the Packers returned to prominence, and have remained there, opponents have seen just how special this place is.

They speak in glowing terms of playing in Lambeau Field; of interacting with the fans (still the best in the NFL); of old friendships with Packers players; of great games and great players; and, yes, of the cold weather that comes in November and December in Wisconsin. I felt that always gave us an edge. Lambeau Field became a tough place to play in late in the year.

The highlight and privilege of my football career was as executive vice president and general manager of the Green Bay Packers. It was an honor to be able to work for such a marvelous organization and in such a hallowed place. The Packers remain the crown jewel of the NFL, and I consider myself very fortunate to have been able to be a small part of its resurrection.

PROLOGUE

IT STARTS WITH the stories. It always starts with the stories. In the sports world, there may be no better storytellers than ex-NFL players. Maybe it's because they spend months smashing against one another in practice, or biding their time on the road, or bonding in their misery during another interminable meeting. But football players always have great stories to tell.

Maybe it's the travel or the emotional and physical toll every game takes on players, all of whom know the next play could be their last. A wrecked knee, a shattered shoulder, one more concussion, and, they all know, a career could be over.

So every player relishes every moment they spent in the game they love and respect and, yes, sometimes fear.

That's where those stories come from. Deep down and, oh so personal, they remember everything and everyone from the game that dominated their lives. The timeframe of particular games may fade, and details aren't always clear, but they remember the plays that matter and they remember the guys they played with.

They are grand, verbose, richly crafted tales of days gone by when the NFL was a different game. Are those stories embellished? In some cases almost certainly they are. But so what? The stories paint a picture of a time that will likely never be seen again, and they exist only in the minds and imaginations and flowery phrases of the guys who were there.

"That's the great thing about football," says Tim Krumrie, the All-Pro nose guard from the Cincinnati Bengals, whose freak play on a warm September afternoon in 1992 at Lambeau Field changed the course of a franchise. "You love to share those stories with players and fans. And there are always great stories."

Yes there are, and that's the point of this book. These stories, told in a way that only the guys who were there could remember and tell them, paint the best picture possible of how the game was played.

"I've got a thousand stories," notes Bob Lurtsema, who played for the New York Giants, Minnesota Vikings, and Seattle Seahawks back in the 1960s and '70s.

Then he laughed.

"Most of them I can't tell you," he added.

But he did relay how the NFL was a true fraternity when the game was played six months out of the year, and when training camp really was used to get players in shape and NFL salaries were such that most players needed an offseason job.

He talked about his great friend, the late Hall of Famer Packers guard Fuzzy Thurston, whom Lurtsema collided with for the first time as a rookie when Thurston was in the final season of his epic career.

He remembers how Thurston complimented him on how he played and how Lurtsema, the wide-eyed clueless rookie, believed it.

"Then I saw the game film the next day," Lurtsema said, laughing. "I was terrible."

But through the crucible of football, the two men became close friends.

"I remember I got 400 tickets for Fuzzy for an event I emceed," Lurtsema said. "Then he turns around and sells them for $330 a ticket. I said, 'Fuzzy, what the hell are you doing?' But that was Fuzzy."

In the offseason, they sold time share properties together in Florida and surely shared the stories only two former players could share.

"We had a great relationship," Lurtsema said, pausing. "I miss him every day."

For me, getting the stories to put into this book wasn't the hard part, but, admittedly, finding the players to tell those remarkable tales in the first place, well, sometimes that was a struggle. Then again, anything worthwhile is worth the struggle.

To that end, I offer my heartfelt thanks to all those people who told the stories, and the people who helped me find those people. In both cases, they didn't know me from a hole in the wall but still took the time to help.

It started with Paula Pasche of the Oakland Press in Michigan and John McFarland in Dallas, Texas, both of whom provided the names and contact information for players that allowed me to begin this rather remarkable journey.

From there, one connection usually led to another, and another after that. Eventually, a collection of player names with their disparate and often wonderful stories about their days in pro football coalesced into a book that is different from any other I've written.

Thanks also to the media departments of several NFL teams, including the Tampa Bay Buccaneers, Detroit Lions, Minnesota Vikings, Washington Redskins, along with Aaron Popkey and Katie Hermsen of the Green Bay Packers. They all provided valuable assistance finding players who, in some cases (and as I suspected), probably never wanted to be found.

Special thanks also to Andrew Howard of the NFL Network, as well as the communications folks at the National Football League Players Association and the NFLPA's Alumni Association, all of whom provided invaluable help and helped me track down a number of players. It is appreciated.

I'd also like to thank former Chicago Bears safety Doug Plank, the No. 46 in the vaunted and infamous "46 Defense" created in the late 1970s by then-Bears defensive coordinator Buddy Ryan. Opponents over the next few years, including the Green Bay Packers, would feel the full fury of that defensive scheme that helped the Bears create perhaps the most dominant defense the NFL has ever seen.

Doug retired before seeing that defense at its rampaging best in 1985, when the Bears took home, to date, their only Super Bowl title. But Doug has stayed close to the game and to his old teammates, and was a huge help in finding other Bears from the 1980s to speak to. He also provided some great insight on his own. I'm not sure how far I would have gotten without Doug's help, so thanks again for that.

Another terrific source was former San Francisco 49ers linebacker Gary Plummer, who eloquently and hilariously told me some stories that, even after years of writing about the

Packers, I had never heard before. He played for the 49ers late in his career after a decade of frustration with the San Diego Chargers. But he was part of a great Packers-49ers rivalry that lasted four seasons and produced some of the most memorable games in the history of both franchises. His lyrical view of playing against the Packers in Lambeau Field drives home again how special that place is on so many levels.

And thanks to all the other players who took the time to speak with me about their memories of facing the Packers. In many cases, they responded to emails or voicemails from out of nowhere, perhaps out of curiosity or maybe a feeling that it was time to tell their stories again.

Asked for fifteen minutes of their time to talk about their memories of playing against the Packers, they often gave twice that and signed off by saying, "If you need anything else let me know," and "Good luck."

Yes, some of the players I'd hoped to talk to said no politely; and, poignantly, two players, whom I had sought for weeks and finally found, declined, saying that their memories simply weren't good enough to remember those days.

One of them paused to consider the offer and then sighed.

"It's just not there anymore," he said of those once-treasured memories of the game he played for years.

Unfortunately, that brought back into stark relief the fact that, as important as the game and the friendships and the stories and the glory might have been, for many former players there is a physical and mental price to pay. And for some players, that bill is coming due. But, for many others, it was a price worth paying.

"I'd do it all over again," Krumrie said, who lives with a fifteen-inch titanium rod in his left leg after a gruesome fractured leg in Super Bowl XXIII.

Finally, I'd also like to thank my new friends at Albion College, who allowed me the time and resources to do the kind of job on this book that was required.

It is a coincidence, I suppose, that Albion College was the place that back in the mid-1950s provided an opportunity to a kid named Fritz Shurmur to play football and baseball, in which he flourished. Shurmur then stuck around for a year as a graduate assistant football coach for a local legend named Morley Fraser and then took over as the team's defensive coordinator until 1961.

Shurmur would go on to a distinguished coaching career at both the collegiate and professional levels, including a stint with the Packers that would include a victory in Super Bowl XXXI in 1996, where he led the NFL's best defense. His name will figure prominently in the memories of several opponents.

And, as always, thanks to my wife, Theresa, who provided valuable advice, support, and more than a few pep talks. She's gotten awfully good at this over the years, and I appreciate it more than she'll ever know.

INTRODUCTION

DAN REEVES LOOKED over in awe at the team on the other sideline and saw what he wanted to be when he grew up.

Back in the mid-1960s, when the National Football League was a far different animal than it is today, Reeves was still just a kid, learning the ways of that raucous and complicated and violent world, and wondering where, and if, he'd fit into it.

He was still a few years from playing in a Super Bowl for the Dallas Cowboys, and years still further away from coaching Super Bowl teams in Denver and Atlanta.

But he saw with his young eyes all those decades ago how the game was really played, and he saw it by watching the Green Bay Packers—the best team and the best organization in football at the time.

He still remembers when his Dallas Cowboys played the Packers in a meaningless exhibition game, when the Packers were at the height of their dominance and potency.

"I remember a pre-season game in 1965, and I was just a rookie," Reeves recalled. "And I remember the thing that got my attention was that on punts their defense stayed on the field. I couldn't believe it. I had (Hall of Fame linebacker) Ray Nitschke on me in a pre-season game, and I had (Hall of

Fame defensive tackle) Henry Jordan on me during the regular season. I said, 'Where is this thing going?' I couldn't believe it. They kept their (starting) offense and defense out there on special teams. That told me a lot. That told me that everything mattered. Everything, no matter how small it seemed."

And that memory has stayed with him through the years, impacting his view of pro football from then on.

"When we played the Packers, we said, 'This is where we wanted to be,'" Reeves said. "It was a great measuring stick."

Those Packers were coached by the already legendary Vince Lombardi, with a roster of players that would one day populate the Pro Football Hall of Fame. But all Reeves could see back then was a coach and a team that took nothing for granted and took a break not even for one play–even in an exhibition game. As a young Dan Reeves, and countless players to follow, would learn, that was how greatness was attained.

And for two seasons, the Cowboys and Packers engaged in epic battles that would help define the modern day NFL and would, in time, allow the Cowboys to become the team it wanted and needed to be.

"The Packers were the best and everyone knew it," Reeves said. "And that's the way they always acted."

The Green Bay Packers have been a part of the NFL since the league's tenuous creation back in the 1920s. One of the original teams located in a small Wisconsin town few people could find even with a map, and named after a meat-packing company *(really!)*, the Packers nonetheless have always been the heart and soul of the league.

And the names have resonated down through the ages: Don Hutson and Curly Lambeau. Vince Lombardi and Bart Starr. Ray Nitschke and Paul Hornung and Jerry Kramer and Henry Jordan and Herb Adderley, and as the years went by, James Lofton and Paul Coffman and Mike Holmgren and Brett Favre and Reggie White.

It has never seemed to stop, and, perhaps more important, it never seems to end.

"Their teams just never seemed to have any weaknesses," said San Francisco 49ers tight end Brent Jones, whose teams battled the Packers for NFL supremacy in the mid-1990s. "They were the gold standard."

And maybe that's what best defines a franchise–when their opponents speak of them with respect and, yes, maybe a little awe.

Perhaps it was the players, who, at some point in their careers when they donned the green and gold, appreciated the significance of playing in Green Bay the most. They could see the impact from both sidelines in a way other players simply could not.

One player with an especially interesting view was fullback Harry Sydney. He was the quintessential journeyman player who battled for everything and, as a result, appreciated it all. He got his first taste of pro football in the upstart United States Football League, playing two seasons for the Denver Gold and one for the Memphis Showboats.

In 1987, he finally caught the NFL's eye and was signed by the San Francisco 49ers, which had taken its place as the league's showcase franchise.

With the 49ers, under head coach Bill Walsh, Sydney learned how to play the game with an accuracy, precision, and dedication to detail that set the 49ers apart from most other teams. In his five seasons with the 49ers, Sydney contributed to two Super Bowl championships.

He was cut by the 49ers during training camp prior to the 1992 season and was immediately picked up by new Packers head coach Mike Holmgren, a former 49ers assistant who was looking for players who knew the right way to play and who understood his offense.

"I saw what Mike was trying to do, and I was excited to be a part of it," Sydney said.

Sydney saw almost immediately that there was no culture of winning in Green Bay, and that had to change.

"It was just little things, really," Sydney said. "You started by calling everyone in the building by their first names. That showed you knew who everyone was, and that their roles were every bit as important as the players and coaches. That's all that mattered."

Putting the pieces in place was Ron Wolf, who had spent nearly his entire adult life as a player personnel director, learning the game at the knee of the American Football League's Al Davis—the often brilliant, always irascible owner of the Oakland Raiders—who enjoyed nothing more than tweaking his more established NFL brethren.

Wolf had watched the 1968 Packers, many of whom were still recovering from the aftereffects of the Ice Bowl win over the Dallas Cowboys a week earlier.

"I really don't know about the Packers," Wolf said. "I didn't pay much attention to them. The guy who ran the team (Davis) didn't think in those terms. He thought much more in terms of what he had to do to better his team and defeat teams like Kansas City, Houston, and San Diego. Especially San Diego. Boy, they had a good team, and so did Kansas City.

"When we played the Packers in the second Super Bowl, we really thought we would have a chance. I remember that second Super Bowl. We were fighting the Vince Lombardi shadow that was all over the National Football League. And without success. We got trounced by the Packers that day."

It was an image Wolf never really forgot, and when the opportunity came in 1991 for him to run his own franchise, he jumped at it.

And the coach he hired, Holmgren, was the maestro. He was a gregarious big man who had the perfect temperament to coach in Green Bay. He understood his role and realized he needed to be as much an ambassador as a coach. He was slow to anger, but when he did the heavens shook.

"A lot of that was orchestrated," Sydney said. "I remember one game Mike was all over the officials, and one of the officials came over to him and said, 'Don't talk to me like that. I'm not one of your players or coaches.' Mike's attitude was that if a player screws up he'd yell at the coaches. But he'd still get on guys all the time."

Sydney played one season for the Packers before retiring, and then in 1995 he was named Green Bay's running backs coach. His depth of knowledge regarding Holmgren's complex West Coast offense was invaluable, and he recounted tales of his experiences with young running backs who tried, and often failed, to grasp what they were supposed to do in that scheme.

One of his favorite stories, and players, was a fast, talented, somewhat misdirected tailback from The Citadel named Travis Jervey.

A special teams demon, Jervey was a free spirit who one time joined with fellow rookie running back LeShon Johnson to purchase a lion.

"Travis was smart as hell," Sydney said. "He could talk about anything—politics, weather, anything. We all loved Travis. He loved the game, but he wasn't *in love with* the game. I remember one time Mike called us up for a pre-game huddle, and we're all ready to go and the tension is building and Mike says, 'Does anybody have anything to say?' Travis says, 'Yeah coach, got any gum?' It was great."

Another running back, Vince Workman, played in Green Bay from 1989 to 1992 before signing a free agent deal with the Tampa Bay Buccaneers in 1993.

"I never wanted to leave," he said. "It was a business decision. I wanted to come back. I wish I'd never left."

Workman got that opportunity to return, and, after retiring in 1996, he was hired by general manager Ron Wolf as a college scout in 1999. In 2001, head coach Mike Sherman made Workman assistant strength and conditioning coach, a position he held for four seasons.

Now out of day-to-day football operations, Workman remains close to the game and to some of his teammates in Green Bay.

"It was a great time," he said. "You talk to a lot of former players, and a lot of them are always coming back to Green Bay. The Vince Lombardi-era guys and guys from the '70s and '80s, they're always coming back. Some guys have even made Green Bay their permanent home. It's a very unique situation."

There have been times when the Packers were awful. But even in those days, when Green Bay was considered a pro football wasteland, there was always something special about the place and the players and the fans.

"Green Bay has always been one of my favorite places to play," said former Detroit Lions defensive end Al "Bubba" Baker. "It was always special to go there, and it was always a good game."

"It was a wonderful experience," said 49ers linebacker Gary Plummer. "Playing at Lambeau Field, I remember thinking that the reality has exceeded the expectation."

"It's hallowed ground," said Chicago Bears safety Doug Plank. "And the more years you play there, the more special the place becomes."

But it was more than just great players, or a great atmosphere, or a great tradition. To play the Packers was to play football in its purest form. The Packers didn't invent the vaunted and feared "Packers Sweep," but they perfected it to the point that, even today, teams can't do it the same way.

They did not invent the forward pass, but with players like Don Hutson and Lynn Dickey and James Lofton and Brett Favre, they took it to places it had rarely gone, and has rarely gone before or since.

And they did not have a lock on home-field advantage, but they knew, as did every opponent who entered the cramped, dingy visitors' locker room, that they were playing a team that did not expect to lose in front of the home folks.

"It would always be a street fight," Plank said. "I think I had more penalties playing against the Packers than any other team I played against. But it was never dirty; it was just always so hard fought. That's just the way it was back then."

But when the game was over, win or lose, opponents often knew what to expect from Packers fans.

"I've never been in a stadium before a game or after that fans have been as nice as Packers fans," Reeves said. "They'd invite you over to have a bratwurst while you're waiting for the team bus. They were great fans. You know you're part of the NFL if you play in Lambeau Field."

What follows is a book unlike most other Green Bay Packers books. Instead of focusing on the iconic players who have made up the franchise, this one looks at the players on the other side of the line of scrimmage, and on the other sideline.

More than a few players over the years probably felt as a young Dan Reeves did. They looked over and saw what they wanted to be when they grew up.

Perhaps no one else can talk about watching the famed Packers Sweep coming right at them than the guys who had to face it. Who better to discuss Brett Favre surveying the field, wide-eyed and ready to make another remarkable play, than the players who dealt with it at that time and in that place? And stories of playing at Lambeau Field in the teeth of Wisconsin winter are the only ones to be believed: the first-hand accounts by those who were there.

To play the Packers in Green Bay was to play in a setting unlike any other. And even hardened veterans who did not play there until late in their careers felt the tug of history. Whether it was staying in a Green Bay hotel in the 1960s with a TV that only got three channels (if the antenna was at the right angle) or players in the 1990s who saw the state of Wisconsin transform on game day, this was an event that even visiting players understood.

"Until you experience it, you don't understand the intensity," Plummer said.

So *Facing the Green Bay Packers* is a chance to hear from those who were there and who can provide a point of view not often available . . . and sometimes almost unbelievable.

Dan Reeves still remembers. And they are memories of a time and a place and a team that he'll never forget and, in truth, never wants to forget.

CHAPTER 1

FACING THE BEST TEAM
IN FOOTBALL

A S THE 1960S dawned, America was changing. Whether it was technology or politics or temperament or attitude, the United States that had been was no longer the country it would be.

Perhaps nothing reflected that more than our sports. Baseball, boxing, and horse racing had been the kings of the American sporting landscape for decades. But as a new decade unveiled itself, that was starting to change. Football, and more specifically professional football, was muscling its way into the national consciousness.

Teams like the New York Giants, Cleveland Browns, Philadelphia Eagles, and Baltimore Colts provided fans with new idols, and their players looked and acted nothing like the stars from the old days. Pro football was born in the 1920s, the brainchild of a few dreamers who saw in football a sport that would tap into something purely American.

And while the NFL did grow, it was a slow, sometimes unsteady, expansion, often plagued by poor attendance, cash

1

flow issues, and the belief among many that the game was simply too violent.

Yet by 1960, perceptions were changing. And another team, one of the originals that had struggled for nearly twenty years and had faced extinction more than once, had risen up the ranks and was capturing national attention.

It was a team from, of all places, Green Bay, Wisconsin. They didn't have a fearsome nickname like Bears or Lions or Giants. They were the Packers, named all those years ago for a local meat-packing company that had provided the financial resources to keep the franchise going in the days when pro football wasn't quite so popular.

In the early years of the National Football League, the Packers had dominated, winning five "world" titles and providing the game's first real superstars, among them Don Hutson, Johnny "Blood" McNally, and Cal Hubbard, while being coached by the irrepressible Curly Lambeau.

But they had fallen on hard times, had not been competitive for years, and had grown nearly irrelevant. Finally, in 1959, a new coach was hired to bring the Packers back from purgatory. Fiery and relentless and uncompromising, his name was Vince Lombardi, and Packers players could see right away he was someone different.

"It's going to be different now," Bart Starr, a veteran quarterback of untapped ability who had struggled under substandard coaching, told his wife after that first meeting with Lombardi.

And it was.

From that point on, the Packers became a force to be reckoned with. They would win world titles in 1961, 1962, and 1965, and they'd also win the first two battles with the American Football League champions in 1966 and 1967, a game that would come to be known as the Super Bowl.

Along the way, the Packers would become the gold standard for what the NFL was supposed to be. It started with a demanding head coach who would push his players so relentlessly that they'd curse his very existence. But they'd also walk through fire for him and ask to do it again, because Lombardi brought out the best in them and made them a team to respect, fear, admire, and strive to emulate.

It featured a quarterback who possessed only average skills but, more important, had an unparalleled gift as a leader and tactician, and whose calm demeanor meant more to his team than an ability to throw a football seventy yards.

The team also featured a defense that, individually, included fine players, but collectively was a defense for the ages, and an offense that wasn't complicated but was nearly impossible to stop.

All told, those Packers teams of the 1960s produced eleven players who would earn induction into the Pro Football Hall of Fame: running backs Jim Taylor and Paul Hornung; linebackers Willie Davis, Ray Nitschke, and Dave Robinson; defensive tackle Henry Jordan; quarterback Bart Starr; defensive backs Herb Adderley and Willie Wood, and offensive linemen Forrest Gregg and Jim Ringo. Lombardi was also inducted, and two other players—guards Fuzzy Thurston and Jerry Kramer—are still awaiting their entry into the Hall that everyone who knows football believes they deserve.

The Packers also featured a home-field advantage unseen before in the NFL, a place to play where the Packers expected to win and, perhaps more to the point, opponents all but expected to lose.

"I remember every time I'd play there I'd look around and I'd think to myself, 'Where are all these people coming from?'" recalls former Chicago Bears safety Doug Plank. "It was less developed back then and Green Bay wasn't a big city, but the place was always packed. And the next day there were motor homes and campers and cars all over the place. It was stunning. They came from all over the place. They showed up from all over the place. These guys are all about football and community. I remember the hotel we'd stay in the night before the game in Green Bay, and in the restaurant we'd be served by someone who looked like your grandmother. It was more than just a football team. It changes the lives for some of these people. It's such a part of their fabric of life."

Of course, it also didn't hurt that in those electric days of the 1960s, the Packers put the best team in football on the field. They won five world titles and changed the NFL in ways that are being felt even today.

"As a fan of the game, I still get goose bumps thinking about it," remembers Brent Jones, former tight end for the San Francisco 49ers, which battled for league supremacy with the Packers in the mid-1990s. "I still think Lambeau Field is the purest of NFL stadiums in terms of legendary franchises. I've become friends with Bart Starr. He was the first professional athlete I followed. I still remember that so well."

FACING THE PACKERS AURA

IT'S NOT DIFFICULT to pinpoint when the Green Bay Packers began their evolution into the dominant team of the 1960s.

It started, as seems all too appropriate, in 1960.

Vince Lombardi was in his second season as Green Bay's head coach, and, after a 7-5 record in his first season in 1959 that had earned him NFL coach of the year honors, he wanted more—a lot more.

And he got it. The Packers posted an 8-4 record, their best since 1944, when they had won their last NFL title. In a season that had seen five teams—the Packers, Chicago Bears, San Francisco 49ers, Detroit Lions, and Baltimore Colts—all vying for control of the Western Conference, the Packers emerged on top in the last week of the season.

That set up the NFL title game between the Packers and the Eastern Conference champion Philadelphia Eagles, at Franklin Field.

In a game dominated by the Packers, the Eagles still came away with a 17-13 win when a last-second Packers drive ended at the Eagles' 10. Famously, after Bart Starr had completed a pass to Jim Taylor to the 10, Eagles Hall of Fame linebacker Chuck Bednarik sat on Taylor and wouldn't let him up until the clock had run out.

"You can get up now," Bednarik apparently told the irate Taylor. "This damn game is over."

The Packers had outgained the Eagles, 401-296, and controlled play most of the day, but Lombardi's decision to go twice for fourth-down conversions deep in Philadelphia territory (which failed) haunted the head coach.

After taking responsibility for those decisions, he told his team afterward that this would be the last playoff game they would lose with him as head coach.

Former Packers linebacker Willie Davis recalls when Lombardi uttered those words, and he thought it was just so much bluster.

It wasn't. In a stunning run through the decade, the Packers won championships in 1961, 1962, 1965, 1966, and 1967 and went 9-0 in that playoff run.

It was perhaps the first real pro football dynasty since the NFL entered its so-called modern era. The popularity of the game, and the men who played it, resonated with American sports fans, who were heading into a time where they wanted something different, something dramatic. The NFL, led by the Packers and such larger-than-life figures as Paul Hornung, Jim Taylor, Ray Nitschke, and, of course, Vince Lombardi, filled that role.

That aura, built slowly after a tough loss in 1960, remains to this day. And NFL players even today, none of whom were even born when the Packers ruled, understand what it means.

"What the Packers and their fans care about is winning," Plummer points out. "For so many other teams, it's about the money. You just don't see that kind of attitude anymore."

Bob Lilly

Defensive tackle/end

His team: Dallas Cowboys 1961-74
His view: Not only were the Packers the best team in football, but they got there by doing it the right way.

WE ALMOST ALWAYS opened our pre-season with the Packers, and I don't think we ever beat them that I can remember. Over the years I got to know a lot of the Packers— (linebacker) Willie Davis and (left tackle) Forrest Gregg, and I got to know (right guard) Jerry Kramer real well. During and after our careers we all stayed in touch. I got to know (quarterback) Bart Starr and (fullback) Jim Taylor pretty well, too. I got to see them at Pro Football Hall of Fame inductions. They were all great guys.

I remember we'd always play them in Dallas in the pre-season, and it was always about 100 degrees and Vince Lombardi worked them pretty good in the heat to see what they could do. That's the way they always were. They'd never take a day off.

I got to know Lombardi pretty well, too. His guys had tremendous respect for him. They all loved him. They were the best-trained bunch of players I'd ever seen. They did not make any major errors. They played a pretty simple offense, but they always had a few special plays, and they were very timely about using them. And it was the timeliness of their play-calling that made them so good. They'd call draw plays when you weren't expecting them.

They didn't do it much, but when they did, it was very effective. Everybody knew their job and everybody was a professional. None of them were dirty, either, because that's just not how they did it. They did their jobs and they did them the right way. Everybody knew their job and everybody was a professional.

We had some great games with them. We made them the team of the '60s, just like we made the Pittsburgh Steelers the team of the '70s.

Lem Barney

Cornerback

His team: Detroit Lions 1967-77
His view: The Packers made the Central Division the toughest in football.

THEY JUST HAD so many great players. It was just a joy to play against them, because they always played the right way. I really enjoyed playing in the Central Division, and I loved studying film. It was a tough division to play in, and that was because of the Packers.

But after Coach Lombardi left, they struggled. They didn't have the same type of coaches, and they weren't drafting the players Lombardi would have drafted. The power shifted over to the Minnesota Vikings and (Coach) Bud Grant. Grant was the quiet Lombardi. I don't think he ever had a bad thing to say.

Lee Roy Jordan
Linebacker

His team: Dallas Cowboys 1963-76
His view: The Packers always made the most of playing in front of their home crowd.

LAMBEAU FIELD WAS really something special, and we always knew how tough they were to play there. It was a great home-field advantage they had, and it was a great home-field crowd. It was unbelievably vibrant. Even in the cold weather, they'd clap with their gloves on. Very devoted fans, and the Packers always played well in front of them.

Tom Matte
Running back

His team: Baltimore Colts 1961-72
His view: Losing to the Packers in the 1965 playoffs still stings.

FACING THE GREEN BAY PACKERS

FIRST OF ALL, of course, they had a great coach in Vince Lombardi. They were very well organized. They had a team you had to respect, and we did. We had some great games against them. That 1965 playoff game is the one I remember most. That game pissed me off. Still does.

(Author's note: The Colts went to Green Bay to face the Packers in the playoffs. Both teams ended the regular season 10-3-1, but the Packers finished first in the Western Conference by virtue of having beaten the Colts twice in the regular season. The Colts entered the game hobbled, as both starting quarterback Johnny Unitas and backup Gary Cuozzo were sidelined with injuries. That left running back Tom Matte to take over. The Packers also lost their quarterback, Bart Starr, to a rib injury on the first play of the game as he tried to make a tackle after a turnover. What followed was a game of survival, with neither team able to gain an advantage, even though the Packers' backup quarterback Zeke Bratkowski threw for 248 yards. In the final seconds of regulation, Don Chandler attempted a game-tying 22-yard field goal, and his reaction after the kick signaled to most Colts that he had missed the kick wide left. But officials called it good, and the game went to overtime, where Chandler won it with a 25-yard field goal. Green Bay went on to beat the Cleveland Browns the next week to win the NFL championship—which would prove to be the first of three straight for the Packers.)

When Unitas and Cuozzo got hurt, there was nobody left, but (head coach) Don Shula had a lot of confidence in me.

I was a jack-of-all-trades but a master of none. I played running back, fullback, quarterback, defensive back, wide receiver, whatever needed to be done. And Unitas taught me how to read defenses.

Unitas was more than instrumental in helping me design an offensive system that would work against the Packers defense, and we were very successful with it. It really upset the apple cart. The Packers defense was really getting upset. I'd do a quarterback draw and take three steps back and run through the hole. It kept them off balance. They didn't know what was happening, and neither did we. But we rose to the occasion.

We went up there and played one heck of a game. It was a very tight game. Of course, that Chandler field goal (which sailed over the left upright) was just no good. Why would the NFL raise the goal post uprights twenty feet the next year and put officials on both sides of the goal post after that? That's my bad Green Bay memory.

But Green Bay was always a fundamentally good team. We knew they were always well-coached and they had a great offense, and they had great players on defense. We always had a lot of respect for Green Bay. It was always a challenge to play them. You got excited playing them because it was always like the Super Bowl.

And the Green Bay crowd was always really into it. It was like playing in Baltimore. The crowd really knew football, and you knew Green Bay was on the rise. Those fans were loyal, dedicated, and they appreciated what the Packers were doing. It was a fun time to play football. It was just a real fun time.

Dave Manders

Center

His team: Dallas Cowboys 1964-74
His view: They were not complicated to prepare for, but they were nearly impossible to stop.

THEY WERE AN easy team to play against for our offense. It was a basic 4-3 defense. Their plan was simple, and they'd say, "Here we are, come and get us if you can." They had a lot of good athletes on that team. I don't know if there were any great athletes, but they were well coached and well disciplined.

I came from Iron Mountain (in Michigan's Upper Peninsula) and I went to Michigan State, so I knew about the Packers, and I always had the highest respect for the Packers long before I got into pro ball. It really grew after Lombardi came there and turned the team around.

I played with (linebacker) Dan Currie at Michigan State and he played for the Packers, and I played with Herb Adderley, who was a year ahead of me at Michigan State. He played for the Packers and then the Cowboys, and I probably had a much higher respect for the Packers than other guys because I was brainwashed. I knew all about them.

Mike Lucci

Linebacker

His teams: Cleveland Browns 1962-64; Detroit Lions 1965-73
His view: Even in their down years, you had to play well to beat the Packers.

GREEN BAY WAS always a great place to go and play. I remember it was in 1965-66 when they were kicking the (crap) out of everyone, but you'd walk down the streets in Green Bay, and people were happy you were there. It was a great place to play. It was more like a college experience.

I remember in the later years when they weren't quite as good as they had been, you always thought that you really had to play great to win a game up there. I remember in 1970, we had a really good team and we blew the Packers out both times we played them, but it was always a good game. You respected who you were playing, and they respected who they were playing.

Bob Lurtsema

Defensive tackle/ Defensive end

His teams: New York Giants 1967-71; Minnesota Vikings 1971-76; Seattle Seahawks 1976-77
His view: The Packers-Vikings rivalry was every bit as tough and memorable as the Packers-Bears rivalry.

I REMEMBER MY ROOKIE year in 1967 and I'm playing for the New York Giants, and I'm going against (Packers all-star guard) Fuzzy Thurston. I mean, *it was Fuzzy Thurston.* So we're playing a little, and he says, "Wow, Bob, you're really good for a rookie." And I think, "Oh my God, Fuzzy Thurston knows my first name."

So he talks to me a little bit more during the game, and this is unusual because offensive linemen usually don't talk that much during a game. Defensive linemen talk all the time, but not offensive linemen. The plays he said I was really good at were the ones where I was able to get off the line of scrimmage, so I'm thinking if he's telling me this, I must be playing pretty well.

Then I saw the game film the next day, and I realized just how badly I really played. But that's what Fuzzy did. We became great friends, and he was always my favorite Packer to play against. As soon as we hit on the line of scrimmage the first time, he'd start talking, and he talked the whole game. He was always yakking, always talking. What a great player and what a great guy. I miss him a lot.

14

Fuzzy and I ended up selling real estate together on Marco Island in Florida. Bob Long of the Packers was also down there, and we'd sell real estate. People started calling that part of Marco Island "Packer Road."

I also remember when Gale Gillingham (who took over the following season at left guard after Thurston retired) would tip whether it was going to be a run or pass play. His feet would be parallel for a pass, and his right foot would be three inches behind his left for a run. So one time, a guy on our defensive line gets hurt and I get into the game real quick, and I'm looking at Gillingham's feet and they're parallel, so I knew it was a run. Before I know it, I'm on my back for three seconds, and they're running it right over me.

I know people always say the Packers-Bears rivalry is the best in football. But I have to say the Packers-Vikings rivalry is even better. That border battle is the best. I was five years playing in New York and we'd play the Redskins and Eagles, but that was nothing compared to when the Vikings and Packers played. The fans are so similar and so devoted to their teams, and they were always good games. And it's still a great, great rivalry.

Dan Reeves

Halfback

His team: Dallas Cowboys 1965-72
His view: You had to always play the right way to beat the Packers.

THEY WERE JUST so talented. Coach Lombardi and (Cowboys head coach) Tom Landry were close friends from their years as assistant coaches on the New York Giants staff. They knew each other very well. So when the Cowboys played the Packers, it was always a big game for Coach Landry.

Every time he played Green Bay, it was a big game. He always wanted to beat the Packers, and he always pointed to the Packers as the team we needed to be one day.

Bill Curry

Center

His teams: Green Bay Packers 1965-66; Baltimore Colts 1967-72; Houston Oilers 1973; Los Angeles Rams 1974
His view: Playing for the Packers taught me to love NFL football.

I WAS STUNNED WHEN the Packers drafted me. I was a 212-pound center, and I'd never gotten a letter from the Packers nor spoken to anyone from the Packers suggesting that they were interested in drafting me.

I was drafted as a junior in the twentieth round. I still had another year to play at Georgia Tech, and then I was going into the service. I stayed at Georgia Tech because I needed a year to mature, and I felt I owed it to Georgia Tech.

But I remember it was a Sunday morning, and my brother-in-law called me and he said, "Hello Green Bay Packers." I thought he was kidding. Back then, the NFL Draft was not that big a deal, and I did not even know they were having a draft. I had no idea. He said "Pick up the paper. You've been drafted by the Packers." I just couldn't believe it.

Pat Peppler (the Packers player personnel director at the time) liked to tell this story about me: Vince Lombardi told him, "Peppler, it's two in the morning and I'm tired. I picked nineteen players. Do something humorous with the twentieth." So he did.

The Packers were already one of the best teams in football, and I thought when I went there that it would continue forever. But I was left unprotected in the expansion draft for the New Orleans Saints. And they were so excited to have me they traded me to the Baltimore Colts. Don Shula (the Colts head coach) said he was really happy to have me because of the way I played special teams. Then I became their starting center, and it was a great experience.

I remember when I went back to play the Packers after I left, it was always fun going back there. They were great guys. Except (linebacker) Ray Nitschke—I was afraid of Nitschke. The NFL is where I learned to love playing football. I had grown up and developed in Green Bay, and it was great fun to play for and against them. I honest to goodness loved every one of those guys.

Every time the Colts and Packers played, it was tight and violently contested. What you saw with both teams that other teams didn't have was when you walked in any stadium you think you're going to win. We always thought we could out-physical teams—both the Packers and Colts.

FACING THE GREEN BAY PACKERS

I remember at the time that Lambeau Field was a special place to play, but I really didn't know it because I was too insulated. If there was a religious experience in a stadium, I'd think more of Yankee Stadium. My intention was always to pitch for the Yankees, but I wasn't good enough.

Back when I played, Lambeau Field looked like just an ordinary college stadium. But we took our grandsons back there last December, and it was indeed a religious experience. I get goose bumps thinking about it now. You think about all that history and all the great players who had been there. It is a religious experience in the minds of many people.

FACING BART STARR

THE STATISTICS WERE never anything to marvel at, especially in today's aerial NFL. But in the 1960s, when quarterbacks called their own plays and were needed to manage games rather than dominate them, perhaps no one did it better than Bart Starr, a seventeenth-round draft pick from Alabama whose frustration with the Packers' direction nearly motivated him to give up the game.

Indeed, in his third season, as the Packers skidded to a 1-10-1 record under thoroughly overwhelmed head coach Ray McLean, Starr completed fewer than 50 percent of his passes and threw only three touchdowns to go along with his 12 interceptions.

Starr saw the Packers going nowhere fast and wondered aloud to his wife, Cherry, if it was even worth it anymore. Sensing quickly that McLean, even after just one season, was in over his head, the Packers executive committee fired him and, upon a recommendation from Chicago Bears head coach George Halas, hired the defensive coordinator of the New York Giants—Vince Lombardi.

It took only one meeting with the new coach for Starr to realize everything would be different.

From 1959 through Lombardi's final season in Green Bay in 1967, Starr was the focal point in a 98-30-4 record that included four world championships and a glittering 9-1 playoff record.

Never flashy, always in control, Starr was the perfect quarterback for these Packers. He was Lombardi's alter ego. Both men, strong-willed in their own ways, knew one of them could not succeed without the other.

Opponents often tried to rattle Starr but soon realized it was pointless. To beat the Packers meant taking the game from them, because the guy under center was not going to make any mistake that would make their job easier.

A four-time Pro Bowler who was inducted into the Pro Football Hall of Fame in 1977, Starr retired after the 1971 season and the next year was named Green Bay's offensive coordinator under head coach Dan Devine.

But Starr was never sure he was cut out to be a coach, and, after one season, he left to pursue other interests and to do color commentary for CBS-TV.

But when Devine left after the 1974 season to become head coach at Notre Dame, the Packers executive committee asked Starr, still beloved and still revered by Packers fans, to take over as head coach. Years later, he said coaching the Packers was the biggest mistake of his life, because he broke his own cardinal rule: he took a position for which he wasn't prepared.

In eight seasons as Green Bay's head coach, Starr managed one playoff berth and an overall record of 52-76-2. He was finally fired after the 1983 season, and, after a misbegotten attempt to start a new United States Football League franchise in Arizona, he stepped away from football altogether.

Still, there are several former players of his who insist that, if Starr had been given another season or two, he would have turned the Packers around.

In the years to follow, he has remained one of the Packers' great ambassadors, even after a stroke in 2015 slowed him down.

But even then, despite his major physical limitations, Starr was on hand at Lambeau Field in November when Brett Favre's number was retired by the Packers.

"The most incredible thing I've ever seen," said Steve Mariucci, Green Bay's quarterbacks coach under Mike Holmgren. "He was not going to miss that moment for anything. He had promised Brett he'd be there, and he was going to keep that promise."

Roger Brown

Defensive tackle

His teams: Detroit Lions 1960-66; Los Angeles Rams 1967-69
His view: Sacking the Packers quarterback seven times in front of a national TV audience on Thanksgiving showed that, at least for one day, the Lions were the better team.

EVERY THANKSGIVING DAY the Lions played the Green Bay Packers. That was the only game on national TV and on radio. It was the only game being played in the country. Not like it is today. It was also a rivalry game, and we were always ready to do battle with them. It was always a great game.

As you know, it's automatic knowledge that Vince Lombardi was quite the taskmaster. He was a great coach, and when you got ready for the Packers and that offensive line of theirs, you had to be ready. It turned out that in the early '60s, the Packers evolved into the team to beat.

I remember in 1962 we played them up there in Green Bay, and I think they beat us, 9-7, and we thought we had outplayed them.

So when they came to Detroit for the Thanksgiving game that year, we were loaded for bear. We were out to show them we were a better team than they were. *(Author's note: The Lions won the game, 26-14, and the defense sacked Starr 11 times, with Brown getting credit for seven. Lombardi later said that was the worst loss in his years as Green Bay's head coach.)*

If we'd played like that against every other team we played, we'd have won the championship. As far as Detroit was concerned, we considered that our home field. We considered that everybody in the nation was watching that game, and we wanted to play the best we could because that's when All-Pro selections were chosen. You could negotiate a better salary. There were a lot of things we had to prove to ourselves. And No. 1 was that we were the better team.

Lee Roy Jordan
Linebacker

His team: *Dallas Cowboys 1963-76*
His view: *Underrated, always prepared, he was the ideal quarterback to run the Packers offense of the 1960s.*

HE WAS AN astute quarterback. He'd use audibles when he thought he had an advantage. He was always prepared, and he was a great leader. Lombardi always selected the players for what he wanted to do, and Bart was the perfect quarterback for what he wanted to do. He managed the team, and he never made mistakes. I mean, Bart was the MVP of the first two Super Bowls, and what were his numbers (combined 29 for 48, 390 yards, three touchdowns and one interception)? It was a different game back then, and he was just such a good manager.

Lem Barney

Cornerback

His team: Detroit Lions 1967-77
His view: Starr was his favorite quarterback from the time he was a kid, and the opportunity to face him as a pro was a dream come true.

IN HIGH SCHOOL I was a Bart Starr fan, because I played quarterback. I'd always watch the Lions and Packers play the Thanksgiving Day game in Tiger Stadium, and I always dreamed of being drafted by the Lions or the Packers. I went to Jackson State (in Mississippi) in 1963 as a quarterback, and I wanted to be just like Bart, because I really admired him.

So I was drafted in the second round by the Lions, along with (running back) Mel Farr, and I had a chance to play against

Bart Starr. I also admired the late, great Vince Lombardi, and it was just a joy to play against the Packers.

I remember my first pro game was against the Packers, and I remember it as if it were yesterday. The first play from scrimmage, Starr did a reverse pivot and handed off to Jim Taylor for three yards. The second play, because Lombardi loved to pick on rookies, he tried a quick out to (wide receiver) Carroll Dale. I intercepted it and went in for a touchdown. That was just a phenomenal feeling, and I said, "This is going to be easy." But it wasn't. We played them to a 17-17 tie, and I thought it was amazing, because they had so many great players.

Starr and (the Baltimore Colts') Johnny Unitas were my favorite quarterbacks. I loved their moves. But Bart was my favorite because of the way he approached the game. He was a dedicated leader, and I still try to talk with him from time to time. I tell him I'm praying for him.

Bill Curry

Center

His teams: Green Bay Packers 1965-66; Baltimore Colts 1967-72; Houston Oilers 1973; Los Angeles Rams 1974
His view: I'd do anything to protect him.

PLAYING FOR BART, for me, was like putting my head in the huddle and seeing Mount Rushmore. It was like that with (the Colts' quarterback) Johnny Unitas, too. I wasn't going to let anybody touch them. I'll tackle them if I have to. With Bart, it was like being in the presence of God. If I ever displeased him, I was crushed.

I remember the playoff game in 1965, when we beat the Colts on that last-minute field goal by Don Chandler. I still run across some of the Colts from that game even now, and they still say that kick was no good.

I still don't know if it was good or not. I snapped the ball, and then I was under a pile and my face was in the mud. But Bart was the holder and he said it was good, and that was good enough for me.

Mike Lucci

Linebacker

His teams: Cleveland Browns 1962-64; Detroit Lions 1965-73
His view: He was the perfect fit for those Packers teams.

HE WAS VERY accurate, and he read defenses very well. He had that sweep, and that weak side play he'd run all the time with (Paul) Hornung and then (Donny) Anderson running it. He was a perfect fit for them. He was cerebral, and he managed the game as well as anybody I've ever seen. For example, he'd run that sweep two or three times and then, boom, he'd hit that slant for a big gain. He always got the job done.

Tom Matte

Running back

His team: Baltimore Colts 1961-72
His view: Calm, cool, and collected, yet Starr didn't abide dropped passes.

BART STARR WAS always so calm, cool, and collected. But I do know he was a lot like my quarterback, Johnny Unitas, and Bart didn't like it when his receivers dropped the ball. But he had some great receivers, and they didn't do that very often.

FACING THE PACKERS SWEEP

IT WAS PERFECTION in its simplest form, and a most devastating level of domination that the NFL had never seen to that date. It wasn't complicated, but under Coach Vince Lombardi it was the Packers' signature play. It was the play that would define the Packers, good or bad.

"We'd run it over and over and over," guard Jerry Kramer recalls. "And it was the opponent's job to stop it. Most teams couldn't, even though they knew exactly what was coming."

Since its inception, football teams have run this most basic, elemental play. You'd run the ball to the left or right, away from the surging line of scrimmage and hoping to turn the corner for a long run. It became known as a "sweep," and every team had at least one version of it.

It is said that, when he was hired as Green Bay's head coach in 1959, Vince Lombardi's first order of business was to find running backs who could make his sweep work. More important, he was intent on making sure he also had the linemen who were quick enough, fast enough, and smart enough to make it work. Because, as Lombardi always knew—and as his teams and opponents eventually figured—all the pieces had to work in harmony if the sweep was to work. No team before or since has been so intricately connected, or performed it as well, as the Packers.

Kramer, the Packers all-star guard, remembers that there was no detail too small for Lombardi when it came to running his "Packers Sweep."

27

Lombardi cared little that every team knew it was coming, and that it would be coming multiple times, during a game. He had so much confidence in his players' execution of the sweep that it didn't matter to him that every opponent knew it.

The play required the guard and tackle to get out of their three-point stances quickly, get to the corner, and make their blocks, ideally creating a lane for the running back to navigate. Having linemen like Hall of Famers Forrest Gregg and Fuzzy Thurston, as well as Kramer and, later, Gale Gillingham, making blocks for the likes of Jim Taylor, Paul Hornung, Donny Anderson, and Elijah Pitts allowed that play to take on something of mythic proportions, even though it didn't succeed as often as history suggests.

The play became so well known throughout football that Lombardi was even convinced to do a film tutorial on the sweep, explaining it to the layman as best he could, though he often lapsed back into his legendary "coachspeak."

But, as with most things, the Packers Sweep changed over the years. Lombardi moved on, and the players who made it work retired. Passing became the primary way to move the ball, and the Packers Sweep now lives mostly in memory.

Roger Brown

Defensive tackle

His teams: Detroit Lions 1960-66; Los Angeles Rams 1967-69
His view: It really wasn't a great play, but the Packers always ran it so well.

IREMEMBER THE CENTER was Jim Ringo, and I remember the guard in front of me was Fuzzy Thurston. He was a great player. I remember Fuzzy was hurt one year, and this rookie came in and did a good job. And then of course, there was the other guard who was Jerry Kramer, and Marv Fleming was the tight end. And, of course, Paul Hornung, Bart Starr, and Jim Taylor; that's etched in everybody's minds.

They ran that sweep quite effectively. You knew it was coming, and our goal was to contain them. The goal was to keep them inside, and (middle linebacker) Joe Schmidt and (defensive end) Alex (Karras) and I would clean them up.

You've got to realize that I don't think that sweep they had was that outstanding a play, but they just whipped the hell out of everyone with it. There were a lot of low scores back then, especially when the Packers played Detroit. When they did run the sweep, it was usually in a situation where we were ready to stop them. But they ran it very well, so you had to cover your spots. If anybody came in my side, they were mine.

It was always a challenge. You had to get up for anything you got, because no one was going to give you a damn thing, and so you had to be ready.

Bob Lilly

Defensive tackle/end

His team: *Dallas Cowboys 1961-74*

His view: Featuring quick and smart linemen, no one ran the sweep as well as Green Bay.

EVERYBODY IN THE league did it, but not as good as the Packers. I guess personnel had something to do with it. They didn't give things away. A lot of teams would pull their guards, but the Packers guards (Jerry Kramer and Fuzzy Thurston, and, later, Gale Gillingham) were quick and smart, and they didn't make stupid mistakes.

I could tell when they were going to do it because they'd zone block me, and they'd put pressure on their fingertips and they'd turn red. So I knew it was coming, but you still couldn't really stop it. It's like a sixth sense. You can smell a rat, but they didn't give away many rats.

⬤

Mike Lucci
Linebacker

His teams: Cleveland Browns 1962-64; Detroit Lions 1965-73
His view: Once the ball was snapped, you knew instantly when the sweep was coming.

THEY RAN SOME basic plays and then they would play-action off of them, and those plays were more of a concern. They'd run the sweep and that weak side play. Then they'd fake it and hit (Boyd) Dowler or (Max) McGee on a slant, or the tight end downfield in the seam. It got to the point where I'd almost wish they'd run that sweep, rather than run it and fake those other plays. But they did run the sweep very well. You didn't always know when they'd run it, but once the ball was snapped, you knew. And it was because of that offensive line. I mean, how many of those guys are in the Hall of Fame? You look at that line and they could run any play they wanted to. It was that good. The sweep was a great play, but they were successful because of the caliber of player they had.

Lee Roy Jordan

Linebacker

His team: Dallas Cowboys 1963-76
His view: They didn't run many plays, but they ran them all to near perfection.

THEY RAN JUST a few plays, but they ran them to perfection. Everybody had an assignment, and I guarantee you with Coach Lombardi everybody did their job. There was perfection in every play they ran. They executed to the nth degree. And they ran it over and over and over again. They didn't think anybody could stop them, and they were right.

Lem Barney

Cornerback

His team: Detroit Lions 1967-77
His view: It was all but unstoppable.

WHAT DID I think of the Packers sweep? When I saw it coming I'd say, "Hail Mary, full of grace, the Lord is with thee." When I saw that train coming, it was fearful. But you had to get through it. You had to cut on the interference, because that was part of my job. It wasn't fun, but that's what I had to do. And Green Bay was the best at it.

When they'd put the wide receiver nine or ten yards out, you knew it was coming, and you had to deal with it.

Facing Vince Lombardi

SOMEWHERE BETWEEN REALITY and legend and myth, Vince Lombardi stopped being viewed as the very real, very flesh-and-blood human being that he was. To former players, to opponents, and to those players who have followed in the years after Lombardi's untimely death in 1970, his name has reverberated down the generations. And, along the way, he morphed from a man into a monument.

To those who played for him, Lombardi was more than a coach. He was a father figure, a mentor, a taskmaster who got more out of players than they imagined they could get from themselves. And the results, in the form of five championships in the 1960s, were there for all to see.

To opponents, he was the coach who pushed all the right buttons at all the right times. He was an innovator, to be sure, but one with his feet planted firmly in the early traditions of the NFL, where running the football and playing tough defense were the keys to winning most games.

He turned Bart Starr from a doubt-ridden, below-average quarterback into a leader who would earn a spot in the Hall of Fame and earn MVP awards for the first two Super Bowls.

He re-directed a halfback, Paul Hornung, who had grown disillusioned after two years of losing with bad Packers teams, making him the centerpiece of a new offense. And he thrived.

Some players he kicked in the butt. Others he patted on the back. Still others he patted on the back while kicking them in the butt. And, somehow, he found the right mix for each player. Lombardi would question their toughness and their dedication and, sometimes, their manhood, and he made them love him for it.

It didn't always work, and Lombardi's actions sometimes left wreckage in its wake.

Bud Grant recalled to Robert Klemko from MMQB.SI.com recently about winning his first game as the Minnesota Vikings head coach in 1967, beating the Packers, 10-7, in Milwaukee.

"We beat them in a very close game, and I think we only threw for about 80 yards, played good defense, ran the ball, got a couple breaks, and won," Grant said. "After the game we're walking off the field. I've always shaken hands after games, but your heart's not in it. It's a ceremony. So I put my hand out, and he wouldn't even shake hands with me. And that was the last time I ever talked to him."

Indeed, Lombardi could be petty and deceitful and childish. He could lose his temper at the worst time for the least important of reasons, and he could hold grudges forever.

For example, he seethed in 1965 when City Stadium was renamed Lambeau Field for the team founder and its first legendary coach, Curly Lambeau. Lombardi, a devout Catholic, was furious that the stadium would be named for a man whose marital infidelities were the worst-kept secret in Wisconsin. Lambeau's moral lapses, at least in Lombardi's view, were reason enough to keep him from attaining such an honor.

Besides, he thought to himself, the stadium should be named after *him* and for what he had accomplished in bringing the Packers back from a football wasteland.

Instead, Highland Avenue, which ran right past the stadium, would eventually be renamed for the coach and, as perhaps the ultimate honor, so would the NFL trophy that would go to the Super Bowl champion.

His players knew all the stories and all the idiosyncrasies of their tortured leader. But to them, or at least to most of them, all that mattered was that Lombardi helped them grow as football players and, more important, as men. And many of the players he treated the harshest in the old days defend him to this day.

"I never would have succeeded the way I did without Coach Lombardi," said right guard Jerry Kramer.

Lombardi was no monument. He was no icon. He was just a man, imperfect as everyone else, who found a way to get more out of football players than perhaps any other coach in history. And maybe that's testament enough.

Bob Lilly

Defensive tackle/end

His team: Dallas Cowboys 1961-74
His view: His philosophy was to do five things well on offense and you'd win.

TOM LANDRY HAD worked with Lombardi in New York, and he always talked about how meticulous he was. They did have different theories about the game, but he always respected how Lombardi approached the game.

I think Lombardi thought if you could do five things really well on offense and throw in a few surprises, you could win. And it worked.

He always got the players that he believed could run his system, and he was loyal to those guys. It was impressive to see.

Mike Lucci

Linebacker

His teams: Cleveland Browns 1962-64; Detroit Lions 1965-73
His view: He was one of those opposing players who knew Lombardi was the kind of coach he wanted to play for.

I GOT TO KNOW (Packers tight end) Ron Kramer and Paul Hornung, and I heard all the stories about Lombardi. He had a way to push buttons, and while he was tough, he was not as tough on Hornung for some reason. He had the ability to chew your ass out and then give you a hug.

He had his favorites and that's for sure. But I always knew this about Lombardi—he looked like a guy you wanted to play for. The way he got his teams to play so well and so smart. He got more out his players than I think I've ever seen a coach do. I wanted to play for him.

Dave Manders

Center

His team: Dallas Cowboys 1964-74
His view: We learned a lot about playoff football playing the Packers in back-to-back years.

WE JUST WANTED to play our best against them. We told ourselves if we don't make any mistakes against them we can win. And that's how you had to play them. They were just so well coached, you couldn't make mistakes. We just thought, wherever the chips fall, let them fall. But Lombardi had his team so prepared to play, it was incredible.

I remember when we played the Packers in the playoffs in 1966 (in Dallas), we really didn't even know who we were at that time. We were just on the cusp of being playoff contenders, and we just wanted to give it our best shot. The next year (the Ice Bowl in Green Bay) it was an attitude of "We've got to do it this year." We never knew when we'd get another opportunity. We just put too much pressure on ourselves.

That game in Dallas was really something. Don Meredith was our quarterback, and a lot of people don't realize this, but he was a very intelligent guy. He had a 175 IQ.

We fell behind the Packers in that game, 14-0, before our offensive team got on the field. I remember they marched right down the field on us and scored a touchdown. Then, on the kickoff, we fumbled, and Jim Grabowski, their starting fullback, picked up the fumble and ran it in for another touchdown. Can you imagine? A starter and he's playing on the kickoff team? But that's how Lombardi coached. His best players were always out there.

We finally got the ball, and we had first and 10 at around the 26. Meredith comes swaggering onto the field, and he looks at the offensive line. We're young and he looks at us and we're white-knuckled in the huddle. So he looks over at the referee, I think it was Tommy Bell, and he said, "Tommy, give me a timeout."

Tommy Bell looks at him and says, "I can't give you a timeout; you have to run a play."

So just like that Meredith looks at our right tackle, Ralph Neely, and says, "Hey Ralph, look over at the 25-yard-line. Isn't that the girl you were out with last night? How was it?" We all laughed, and then he looks over at the ref and says, "Tommy, we're ready to play." That calmed us all down, and I think we scored on that possession, and it ended up being a terrific game. We lost, but we learned a lot about ourselves.

We played the Packers tough that game, and we knew if we got another opportunity, we had learned so many valuable lessons. And, of course, we did.

Bill Curry

Center

His teams: *Green Bay Packers 1965-66; Baltimore Colts 1967-72; Houston Oilers 1973; Los Angeles Rams 1974*
His view: *It was a complicated relationship that only started to make sense years later.*

I T TOOK ME years to distill the memory of Lombardi. It was very complicated and very traumatic for me.

I didn't like him from the get-go. I had played high school football for a wonderful man. He never screamed at us. He never raised his voice to us. Then I played college football for the great Bobby Dodd. He was a genius. He loved us and he treated us like men. His emphasis was on graduating. He was like a god to me.

Then I got to Green Bay and met Lombardi, and he was not godlike. He was everything I wasn't used to. He wasn't southern and he was Catholic, and I wasn't used to that. And when he showed his disapproval of me, I didn't respond well.

So when we got to Super Bowl III, I was with the Colts, and I was the only player to have played for both Lombardi and Shula. I shot my mouth off to the media that week and said how much I loved how Shula coached and how I had hated playing for Lombardi. I said a few other things, and that didn't go over very well with a lot of the Packers, and I never should have said it.

I ran into Paul Hornung a couple of years later in New Orleans, and he wanted to fight me. He said, "What you said about the old man was wrong." He said that Lombardi would treat you like his long-lost son. And I said, "No, what I said was exactly right." So he wanted to fight me right then and there. It was immature on my part.

So a year or so later, I'm at a presidential prayer breakfast, and guess who's walking down the aisle and coming at me? I was looking for someplace to hide, but I couldn't. But Coach Lombardi comes up to me, and he holds out his hand, and he really does treat me like his long-lost son. I felt about an inch high. He said, "Bill, you and I should have a face-to-face meeting sometime," and I said that was a good idea.

But I procrastinated, and the next thing I know, he was in the hospital dying. Bob Long, one of my former teammates with the Packers, called me and said that we were going to visit him.

Now I wasn't as afraid of Coach as I was of his wife, Marie. I was terrified to see her after everything I'd said. But she saw me in the hospital hallway and embraced me. It was wonderful.

So I saw Coach and I touched his hand in bed, and I said, "Coach, I said some things I shouldn't have said." And he forgave when I least deserved it. I'm eternally grateful to Bob Long for making me go see him. It's something I've never forgotten.

Facing the Lambeau Field Weather

IT'S FUNNY; FEW opposing players paid much attention to the late-season weather in Green Bay until the infamous "Ice Bowl" of 1967.

Prior to that game—which has etched itself permanently into NFL legend because of the fearsome conditions, and not necessarily because of the quality of football—Green Bay weather was hardly an issue.

After all, everyone understood that it did not require a degree in meteorology to grasp the fact that playing in northern Wisconsin in November and December would likely be no picnic. It would be cold, it would likely be windy, and chances were good that ice and snow would not be far behind. You dealt with it, and you moved in because there were no alternatives.

But on December 31, 1967, everything changed. In front of a horrified national TV audience, the Packers hosted the Dallas Cowboys in the NFL Championship Game that redefined what playing in the elements really meant.

On that day, when the temperature dipped to minus 15 (and minus 46 wind chill factor), it was thought by some players and league officials that the game would have to be postponed. But it wasn't, and the game that followed, playing on something akin to an ice rink and which degenerated into a battle for survival, is still revered and analyzed today.

"I watched that game on TV," said San Francisco 49ers linebacker Gary Plummer, who would play against the Packers years later. "I couldn't believe it."

But aside from the result, the game brought to the forefront the impact weather could have on a game and also brought to the consciousness of Packers opponents what playing in Green Bay late in the season can mean.

Indeed, when the NFL schedule for the season is revealed, Packers opponents always go to the closing games to see if they have to travel to Green Bay to play.

"It's a huge home field advantage," said Adam Timmerman, who began his career in Green Bay.

And for teams that do beat the Packers late in the season, it's a badge of honor not only to have won a road game at a tough venue, but to have beaten the Packers in their unique element.

Walt Garrison

Running back

His team: Dallas Cowboys 1966-74
His view: He never knew it could be that cold, and people would still actually come to watch.

THAT'S ABOUT ALL I remember from the Ice Bowl. I've never been in weather that cold before. It was unbelievable. And I was standing on the sidelines most of the time, since I was the kick returner that year.

But I'm sitting there, and Don Perkins, our starting half-back, comes over and sits down next to me. I look at him and say, "Perk, can you believe we're out here?"

Perkins smiles and points his head back to the stands and to all the people who were there watching.

He said, "At least they're paying us to be here." And he was right about that.

●

Dan Reeves

Running back

His team: Dallas Cowboys 1965-72
His view: Never been that cold, and have never been that cold since.

YEAH, I THINK everything about that (Ice Bowl) game has been covered from A to Z.

I guess about a million now say they were there, but I know that the stadium was full. I couldn't believe it. I was there but I had to be there, and I wondered what so many people were doing there. I remember I had my hands as far down in my pants as I could. I'd never been that cold before, and I've never been that cold since.

I also remember this. When I was coaching the Atlanta Falcons, we played the Packers at Lambeau Field—I think it was the first game of the season—in 2002. Everybody talks about the cold weather at the end of the season, but it was so hot up there for that game. I think they said it was a record-high temperature for that day (it was close, 91 degrees). It was really uncomfortable.

We lost that game in overtime, but then we went back there for the playoffs in January, and it was cold and snowing and we beat them. I think that was the first home playoff loss in team history, so that was pretty special. *(Author's note: It was—the Packers had gone 13-0 in playoff games in Wisconsin since 1933. They were 11-0 at Lambeau Field and 2-0 in Milwaukee before that 27-7 loss.)*

So I've been there for one of the coldest games, and I've been there for one of the hottest.

Bob Lilly
Defensive tackle/end

His team: Dallas Cowboys 1961-74
His view: He was amazed by the fans who actually showed up to watch.

I HAD A GREAT deal of admiration for everyone who went to that Ice Bowl game. I remember thinking, "Man, these people are tough." I also remember there were these three guys behind, in the third or fourth row up, with no shirts, no coats, no nothing, and they were drinking out of a pint bottle. And that was before the game had even started. I couldn't believe it. I told my teammate George Andre, "These people are going to die."

So I looked back up there during the game to see what had happened to them, and those guys were gone. I wondered if they really had died. But no, they came back and they had even put coats on. We were pretty uncomfortable.

Jeff Siemon

Linebacker

His team: Minnesota Vikings 1972-82
His view: Playing in the cold always provided an incentive and an advantage.

ACTUALLY ENJOYED PLAYING in the cold weather. I grew up in Bakersfield, California, where it was always 100 degrees. I hated the heat. I felt I had more energy in cold weather, and I think we always felt we had more of an advantage in cold weather. The Packers probably thought the same thing.

(Vikings Coach) Bud Grant always preached that we should be impervious to the cold. Just do your job, and the other team will be thinking about how cold it is. Of course, that didn't quite work when we played in Green Bay. We were both northern teams and we were accustomed to playing in the cold, so we were both just able to play the game and not think about the weather. We both had great historical traditions. We both had unique fan bases, and both were very supportive of their teams. I don't think the fans ever thought about the weather, either. That's just what you expected up there.

Doug English

Defensive end/Defensive tackle

His team: Detroit Lions 1975-85
His view: *Playing in the Green Bay cold was simply a matter of survival.*

THERE IS ONE game that stands out in my mind. It was in December in Green Bay, and at the kickoff it was minus 6. It had been snowing all week in Green Bay, and they had the field covered. But before the game they plowed off all the snow, and then they took the cover off and painted the field green. There was just a little grass in the corner, but that was it for the grass. They made it look nice for the TV cameras.

Then that Saturday night before the game, it snowed some more—another six inches or so. They didn't have time to plow it, so they just turned on the heating coils under the field. It melted the snow into mud. So it was minus 6 and the wind chill was ridiculous, something like minus 20, and we were playing in the mud.

During the game, I pulled the front of my jersey out and used it so I could try and keep my hands warm. Then I noticed after a TV timeout that my jersey had frozen into the shape of my hand. When I pulled my jersey back down, it crunched.

Obviously, they were more used to the cold weather than I was, but it was almost like survival playing in that cold. There were some brutal ones, but when you survived them those are the things you're most proud of. Fortunately, we usually caught them in Green Bay earlier in the season when it was warmer.

Facing Linebacker Ray Nitschke

THE LIST OF great Green Bay Packers defensive players runs long and impressively. It starts from the team's earliest day, when guys with names like "Jug" and "Buckets" roamed the field, and has continued ever since.

But it was in the 1960s when, not coincidentally, the rise of the Packers in the standings coincided with a legion of wondrous defenders who included players like defensive tackles Henry Jordan and Ron Kostelnik, ends Lionel Aldridge and Willie Davis, linebackers Dave Robinson and Lee Roy Caffey, and defensive backs Willie Wood and Tom Brown.

But one defender epitomized the Green Bay Packers more than all the others. He even had the perfect name to reside in the middle of the Packers' great defenses.

Ray Nitschke.

His bald head, his missing front teeth, his gravelly, thunderous voice, his aura of mayhem made the Packers middle linebacker not only the perfect symbol of Green Bay's rugged defense, but the image of a new and growing NFL. He was one of the faces of a league that placed a premium on sheer, unapologetic violence—and the fans ate it up.

Amazingly, Nitschke as a kid had hoped to play quarterback at the University of Illinois. But injuries on the defense forced Nitschke to linebacker, where he flourished. In 1958, the Chicago native was the third-round draft of the Green Bay Packers, a crushing disappointment, since he dreamed of playing for his hometown Bears.

But it wasn't until Vince Lombardi was named Green Bay's head coach that Nitschke began to make his mark. He took over at middle linebacker in 1960, where he remained until he retired in 1972.

In the intervening years, he earned a reputation as one of the toughest, smartest, and meanest linebackers in a league filled with such forces of nature. Indeed, Lombardi's view of Nitschke grew exponentially early in his career when, during a practice, a metal tower fell on the linebacker.

Telling his players that Nitschke was fine and that everyone should get back to work, Lombardi only found out later that a jagged piece of metal had actually pierced Nitschke's helmet and just missed his skull. But Nitschke had listened to his coach and returned to practice. The helmet, with the hole circled in red, remains on display in the Packers Hall of Fame, a testament to one of the game's toughest guys.

He rubbed many teammates the wrong way during his playing days, with running back Paul Hornung admitting the two never got along and rarely spoke. But even Hornung admitted there were few more intimidating players in the NFL at the time.

Nitschke anchored a defense that led the Packers to five world championships. He finished his Packers career with 25 interceptions, and his 20 career fumble recoveries remains second in team history behind Willie Davis. He was a five-time All Pro and a Pro Bowler in 1964, and he was named to the NFL's 50th and 75th Anniversary teams.

Nitschke was inducted into both the Pro Football Hall of Fame and the Packers Hall of Fame in 1978, and in 1983 his iconic No. 66 was retired, one of just six numbers retired by the team (Reggie White's No. 92, Bart Starr's No. 15, Don Hutson's No. 14, Brett Favre's No. 4, and Tony Canadeo's No. 3 are the others).

Soft-spoken and polite off the field, Nitschke walked through town in his black-rimmed glasses that made him look more like a high school science teacher than a ferocious football player. He was well known for his love of kids and of the Green Bay community, which he made his permanent home after he retired. In fact, he insisted on having his home phone number listed in the Green Bay phone book.

He was so popular with fans that when a younger player, Jim Carter, stepped in as Green Bay's starting middle linebacker, the blowback was extensive. Carter even admitted years later that he suffered psychologically because fans refused to accept him.

Nitschke continued to live and die with the Packers over the years, and when Green Bay beat the New England Patriots in Super Bowl XXXI, he was seen weeping at the team's victory parade.

Two years later, Nitschke suffered a heart attack and died at age sixty-one. But even today, his memory hovers over Lambeau Field, a symbol of the Packers' enduring legacy.

Dan Reeves
Running back

His team: *Dallas Cowboys 1965-72*
His view: *Deceptively quick, he was the leader of a great defense.*

THEY HAD SO many great players on defense, but I think Nitschke was the best of them all. He roamed from one side of the field to the other, and he was just such an aggressive tackler.

He may not have looked it, but he was also a lot quicker than people gave him credit for. You can't make the plays he did without being quick. And we knew that when playing the Green Bay Packers, if you were going to be successful, somebody had to block Nitschke. He was a sideline-to-sideline player, and he was difficult to account for.

Bob Lilly
Defensive tackle/end

His team: Dallas Cowboys 1961-74

His view: Hard-nosed and perhaps a little underrated, Nitschke was the quintessential NFL linebacker.

HE WAS TOUGH and he was hard-nosed, but he was clean. He was just a tough guy to account for, and he was the leader of that defense. I'm still not sure he got the credit he deserved.

Al Baker

Defensive end

His teams: Detroit Lions 1978-82; St. Louis Cardinals 1983-86; Cleveland Browns 1987 and 1989-90; Minnesota Vikings 1988
His view: Playing against Nitschke was overwhelming.

RAY NITSCHKE REPRESENTED everything that the old NFL Central Division was. Hard-nosed, and Green Bay represented that more than any other team. He *was* the Green Bay Packers. Here you are a kid, and you're saying, "Wow, am I really playing in Lambeau Field against guys like Nitschke?" Each one of the games there was a new experience.

And then, on top of that, what I recall more than anything is, "Man, I'm playing at Lambeau," and then there's Bart Starr standing there. It was all pretty amazing to me.

Dave Manders

Center

His team: Dallas Cowboys 1964-74
His view: No front teeth, no hair, but no doubt about his ability.

OH MY GOD, he was just a sight on a cold day. No front teeth. No hair. He looked like he was from outer space.

But what a great player Ray was. He was a lot faster than a lot of people realize, and he was always in on plays. He was the perfect linebacker for the Packers.

Bill Curry

Center

His teams: Green Bay Packers 1965-66; Baltimore Colts 1967-72; Houston Oilers 1973; Los Angeles Rams 1974
His view: I had a better chance of blocking him in games than in practice.

WHEN WE PLAYED the Packers, what always worried me most was Nitschke. I remember when I played for the Packers, he just killed me in practice. I had a better chance of blocking him in games than I did in practice.

My worst days were not Sunday afternoons, but Tuesdays and Wednesdays in practice. He just destroyed me in practice, because he was so much better than me. With the Colts, we had a system of audibles, because I knew what Ray was going to do. I remember I wrote a book with George Plimpton, and I said I used to dominate Nitschke. But that was baloney.

You had so much to worry about with that Packers defense. You had to worry about (defensive backs) Herb Adderley and Willie Wood. You had to worry about Henry Jordan, a defensive tackle who could run like a linebacker. And maybe the best player of all was (linebacker) Willie Davis. Nobody blocked him.

Tom Matte

Running back

His team: Baltimore Colts 1961-72
His view: An intense, funny guy who made football fun.

OH GOD, NITSCHKE was great. I'd line up in the backfield, and he'd point to me and start growling, "I'm gonna kill you, Matte!" I actually started laughing. He was such an intense guy, and funny as hell. You can't take that away from him.

He was a great guy. He could read plays instinctively, and he was always around the ball.

The best linebacker I ever played against was (Chicago Bears) Dick Butkus. He'd just run right through you. Nitschke was the same way. But I still remember looking across at him and his growling at me. I'd just laugh my ass off.

Frozen In Time: The Ice Bowl Revisited . . . Again

Looking back some five decades later, and Dallas Cowboys defensive tackle Bob Lilly is still convinced they should have used a screwdriver.

It is perhaps the most analyzed game in NFL history, and not because of the brutal cold (which seems to get colder with each re-telling) in which it was played.

The facts are etched in history, known by even the most casual football fan of a certain age. As for Packers fans? Well, try finding one who didn't attend the game, and, if they didn't, then their father, brother, sister, mother, aunt, second cousin, or close friend was sitting at Lambeau Field when history was made.

On December 31, 1967, the battered dynasty that had been the Green Bay Packers was showing some cracks. It was an older, injured team that hosted the young, vibrant, and hungry Dallas Cowboys for the NFL Championship. The winner would go on to play the AFL champion in the second installment of a "world championship game" that had recently been dubbed something called the "Super Bowl."

The day before the game, as everyone knows, the weather was seasonably cold, because, after all, it was late January in Wisconsin. What else would it be? But overnight, everything changed. A cold front roared through, dropping the temperature from the tolerable mid-teens to an excruciating 15 below. And, oh yes, the wind chill factor of minus 46 made it also inhuman.

"I really thought the game would be called off," recalls Dallas Cowboys linebacker at the time, Lee Roy Jordan.

Several Packers players also believed the game would be postponed.

And while postponement was, briefly, considered by NFL Commissioner Pete Rozelle, the thought was dismissed. This was, in the final analysis, a championship game, and nothing stopped a championship game.

So the two teams collided on the frozen turf, slipping and sliding their way into NFL lore, in which the chief rival for each may have been not the opponent, but rather the elements.

Packers players were at least used to the cold weather. But for the Cowboys, this was a new, agonizing experience.

"The defensive linemen told me they weren't going to wear gloves because they couldn't get a pass rush," said Jordan, an Alabama native who has since made his home in Texas. "So I said I wouldn't either. After the first series I asked, 'Where are the gloves?' It was really tough on the linebackers and linemen to try and pass rush."

In the end, it was more about survival than victory for both teams, as each tried to navigate a field that grew icier by the minute. (The cold had damaged the field's new underground heating system, the pride and joy of Coach Vince Lombardi. Even so, some Cowboys to this day insist Lombardi had them turned off on purpose to give the Packers an advantage.)

Nevertheless, for this Cowboys team, which was convinced it had reached a par with the powerful Packers, this was another opportunity to prove they belonged.

They'd had an opportunity the year before to go to the first incarnation of the NFL-AFL championship game, when they faced the Packers at the Cotton Bowl in Dallas.

In 1966, the Cowboys faced the Packers for the first time in the NFL title game and played to a standstill. They even had a chance to tie the game, driving deep into Green Bay territory before being turned away on fourth down. They lost, 34-27, but it proved to them that they had arrived.

The next year, they had to face the Packers again, but this time in Green Bay. And the rest, of course, is history.

Lost in history is the fact that this was a battle between the NFL's past and its future. The Packers, in point of fact, had seen their best years in the rearview mirror. Entering this game, the Packers were an old, injured team with a burned-out head coach who had already secretly decided that this would be the last game he would ever coach at Lambeau Field.

The Packers' dominance had made the NFL a marquee national product, and they had done it with a dominant defense, an efficient offense, and a system that was easy to prepare for but nearly impossible to stop.

The Cowboys, still a relatively new franchise with a view toward the future and a different way to be successful, had nearly unseated the Packers the previous year. Now they had another chance against a Packers team that, while still dangerous, was not what it had been.

"I think we had a good team," said halfback Dan Reeves. "But I still think they were better. Until we beat them, they were the better team."

And the Cowboys seemed ready to take that title on the first play of the fourth quarter with a bit of trickery.

"We had been running this particular running play the entire game, and they'd been stopping it," Reeves remembers. "They were doing a great job on it. (Quarterback) Don Meredith called his own plays, and in the huddle he said, 'What do you think of a halfback pass?' and I said, 'Well, they're certainly coming up fast so it could work.' So he called it. I remember I got the ball and looked up and saw (wide receiver) Lance Rentzel was so wide open that the biggest problem was keeping my hands warm and getting the ball to him. I remember the field was frozen, and conditions were getting worse by that point, and it was difficult just to stand up."

The 50-yard touchdown pass from Reeves to Rentzel stunned the Packers and the crowd, put Dallas in front, 17-14, and with the Packers having been stymied offensively the entire second half, it seemed that might be enough.

But then the Packers embarked on their famous final drive, with a huge assist from a relatively unknown running back named Chuck Mercein, staggering toward the Dallas goal line in a final desperate effort to score and win the game.

"That's what great teams do," Reeves aid. "They were very good, I'll tell you."

It culminated with the Packers on the Cowboys' 1-yard line with a chance to run one more play before time would very likely run out on the game—giving the Packers domination of the NFL.

In a final sideline discussion with Lombardi, quarterback Bart Starr suggested he sneak it in. In a piece of sage advice that every Packers fan knows, Lombardi said simply, "Well, run it and let's get the hell out of here." Starr went back to the huddle, laughing at Lombardi's simple advice.

Starr's sneak between center Ken Bowman and right guard Jerry Kramer has become the stuff of legend.

But while it was celebrated by the Packers, it remains a sore point for the Cowboys, who were convinced they were the better team that day.

"We really thought we were, but we didn't prove it," Reeves said. "And that's what you had to do against a team like the Packers. You had to take it from them and we didn't."

Star defensive tackle Bob Lilly remembers that final sequence all too well.

"The Packers were just so well disciplined on that drive," he said. "They ran the perfect plays. And one I remember on the 1-yard line, the Packers called a timeout and we tried to dig in to get some footing, but the ground was frozen. Really and truly, if we'd had any brains at all we would have called a timeout of our own. We had already talked about using a screwdriver and digging a hole and that would have given us a push. Our equipment guy Jack Eskridge was all set to do it, but we didn't do it."

The sneak was what every Cowboys defender expected, and, yet, even knowing what was coming, they could not stop it.

"They did exactly what I would have done," Lilly said. "I absolutely did expect a quarterback sneak and we tried to get as low as we could, but it was like spinning your wheels. (Linebacker) Chuck Howley came over the top and almost got there, but he just couldn't get there. That loss broke our hearts. It was a very tough loss for us, and it affected us into the next year."

Jordan recalls the details, as well, even all these years later.

"I was lined up over the fullback (Chuck Mercein), and I had two responsibilities—tackle the fullback if he got the ball, or tackle the quarterback if he was going to try and sneak it in," he said. "So they double-teamed (defensive tackle) Jethro Pugh, and once Bart took his jab step back, he was over the goal line, and there was nothing we could do about it. Everyone knew it was coming."

Along with the other lore surrounding the game was the belief that the Packers right guard Jerry Kramer, who made the crucial block on Pugh, was offside.

"Sure he was," Jordan said.

"Of course he was," said Lilly. "But it wouldn't have mattered, because we were standing on ice."

In the locker room after the game, both teams were physically and emotionally wrung out. Players wept in agony and relief and disappointment and joy, and a number of Cowboys players, including Lilly and Jordan, admitted they suffered frostbite. Several Packers players did, as well.

To this day, Jordan believes his Cowboys had outplayed the champs, and had the weather been even borderline decent, they would have prevailed.

"I felt like we had the better football team in the Ice Bowl," he said. "We felt we could have won it, but the weather took out one of our best players (wide receiver and Olympic sprinter), Bob Hayes. Bob was allergic to cold weather. He was from South Florida, and he had his hands in his pants the entire game. I think most of our guys got frostbite. I know I did. Even now when it gets below 40 degrees, my hands hurt."

He said those physical problems continued decades after that game.

"I know some guys who had lung problems, and that affected them later in life," Jordan said.

Center Dave Manders, a native of Michigan's Upper Peninsula and who missed the game with an injury, said he caught a cold standing on the sideline that lasted for the next three weeks.

"It was miserable," he said, laughing. "But for a lot of reasons."

Packers quarterback Bart Starr admitted later he had no idea that his team still had another game to play, Super

Bowl II, against the AFL champion Oakland Raiders the following week in Miami, Florida. To Starr, and to most of the Packers, beating the Cowboys was their championship game.

Of course, the Packers dispatched the Raiders, and the exhausted, jubilant Packers carried their head coach off the field. Weeks later, he resigned as head coach to concentrate on his duties as Green Bay's general manager. Less than a year later, bored and frustrated, he resigned that role, too, to take on the task of rebuilding the Washington Redskins as coach and general manager.

Barely a year after that, the great man was dead.

And the Packers, who had dominated the decade, would begin a slide toward mediocrity that wouldn't end for another thirty years.

Meanwhile, the Cowboys used the lessons they learned from the Packers to become one of the NFL's most consistent and talented teams.

"I remember we lost to Cleveland the next two years in the playoffs, but I was convinced the Packers were better than those Browns teams we lost to," Reeves said.

Nonetheless, in the eighteen seasons after the Ice Bowl, the Cowboys reached the playoffs sixteen times, going to five Super Bowls and winning two.

"I'm not sure we could have had that much success without having played the Packers and learned how they played the game the right way," Reeves said. "We always tried to do that."

CHAPTER 2

THE IN-BETWEEN YEARS

THESE WERE NOT the best of times for the once-proud organization.

Vince Lombardi, the architect and patron saint, was dead. The icons of an era had retired. A new breed of player had stepped in, but it was not the same. How could it be? Players like Nitschke and Davis and Robinson and Hornung and Starr and Gregg and Adderley and Wood and Thurston and so many others had retired, and their like was never to be seen again.

To that end, the Packers had been replaced by newer, flashier teams like the Dallas Cowboys, Pittsburgh Steelers, San Francisco 49ers, and Washington Redskins, who played a new kind of football that relied on quick-strike passing, speed, and power.

And while the Packers had not descended into disaster, as the franchise had in the 1940s and '50s, what they had become might well have been worse: they had become simply ordinary.

Indeed, in a span from 1968 through 1991, the Packers had five winning seasons and two playoff appearances. Never awful enough to inspire pity, but never good enough for anyone to get genuinely excited about, the Packers lived in an NFL purgatory, trapped between the darkness and the light.

And not even Bart Starr, the beloved former quarterback who took over as head coach in 1975, could turn their fortunes around.

Highlighted by perhaps one of the worst trades in NFL history perpetrated the season before by Coach Dan Devine, the Packers picked up aging quarterback John Hadl from the Los Angeles Rams in October 1974 and gave away first-, second-, and third-round draft picks in 1975, as well as first- and second-round picks in 1976.

In nineteen starts over the next season and a half, Hadl completed 280 of 537 passes and threw 29 interceptions, 21 coming in Starr's first season as head coach in 1975.

The trade, still reviled by Packers fans as the worst in team history, crippled the franchise for years and forced Starr, who had no previous coaching experience, to start a rebuilding project.

He was never able to do it.

Maybe he had earned plenty of credit for his years as a Packers icon or, almost as likely, the fact that the players genuinely liked playing for him, so Starr was actually given nine seasons to work his magic. In the end, Starr was able to post only a 52-76-3 record that included just two winning seasons and one playoff berth.

In 1984, the Packers again looked to their storied past by hiring Forrest Gregg, the man Vince Lombardi had called the best offensive lineman he'd ever coached, as their new leader.

But under Gregg, the Packers would descend, at least in the view of many NFL observers, into an undisciplined group, the highlight (or lowlight) of which was a nasty ongoing thermonuclear warfare with the rival Chicago Bears.

Struggles on the field soon gave way to problems off the field, too, as several Packers, including beloved wide receiver James Lofton, found themselves deeply involved in legal issues that too often ended up with players not on the field but in the courtroom.

Gregg lasted four seasons, carving out a 25-37-1 record and resigning after the 1987 season to take over the rebuilding of the football program at his alma mater, Southern Methodist University.

But the humiliation only grew for the Packers, who by this stage had managed just four winning seasons in the twenty years since Vince Lombardi had been carried off the Orange Bowl Field in Miami on the shoulders of his players after the Packers had won Super Bowl II.

In that time, four coaches had tried to rekindle the fire, and all had failed.

The last two coaches had been throwbacks to the Packers glory years, so team president Robert Parins and the executive committee charged with hiring a new coach decided on another strategy. They set their sights on a tough, successful college coach, George Perles, who had just taken Michigan State to the Rose Bowl.

And all seemed in order when Packers general manager Tom Braatz received a call from Perles saying he would take the job. But the next morning, Perles called again and said he'd changed his mind and would remain at Michigan State.

For those on the outside looking in, it looked like another slap in the face for the organization. The same franchise that had hired Vince Lombardi now had coaches backing out of opportunities to coach a team that appeared to be going nowhere fast.

Eventually, the Packers hired Cleveland Browns offensive coordinator Lindy Infante as head coach, and, despite a spark of optimism in 1989 when the "Cardiac Pack" pulled out several last-minute wins on the way to a 10-6 record (but no playoffs), the Packers again fell back to mediocrity.

For more than twenty years, the Packers wandered in the NFL wasteland, Nevertheless, incredibly enough, Lambeau Field was still filled to capacity.

"That's the great thing about Packer fans," said former Minnesota Vikings defensive tackle/end Bob Lurtsema, who retired in 1975 after being released by the Seattle Seahawks. "Even when they weren't very good, the fans were always there. I remember one of the worst decisions I ever made. I'd just been released by the Seahawks in the final cutdown, but they said they were going to re-sign me. Then I got a call from a friend of mine, Dave Osborn, who I'd played with in Minnesota, but who had finished his career in Green Bay. He told me, 'Call the Packers in an hour. They want to sign you.' I wasn't sure if he was serious or not, but I thought about it. I never made the call, though, and I wish I had because there's so much history there. Everybody I knew had played in Green Bay, and they really liked it. And the way people embrace that team is nothing short of spectacular."

FACING THE PACKERS OFFENSE

THE PACKERS OF the mid-1980s had an offense good enough not only to reach the playoffs on a consistent basis but, perhaps, challenge for a championship.

The defense? Not so much.

If those Packers were now up for anything, it was that they could score from anywhere on the field with an array of weapons most teams would have envied.

There was quarterback Lynn Dickey, who, when healthy, could go head-to-head with the league's best quarterbacks at a time when throwing the ball was what NFL teams did best.

The pinnacle was 1983, when all the facets of the Packers came together to provide the kind of aerial circus that entertained fans and frustrated opponents.

That season, Dickey threw for 4,458 yards (through the 2015 season, still the second-highest total in team history) and 32 touchdowns. Four receivers—James Lofton (58), John Jefferson (57), Paul Coffman (54), and Gerry Ellis (52)—each caught more than 50 passes, with Lofton averaging an incredible 22 yards per catch. For the season, the offense gained 6,172 yards, the most of any team in the NFL, and scored 429 points, fifth-best in the league.

"We could win with anyone offensively," Dickey said. Unfortunately, although they often piled up points and yards at an astonishing pace, the defense was doing exactly the same.

The Packers defense allowed a staggering 6,403 yards, again the most in the league that year, still a team record, while allowing 439 points.

Many Packers from that era still wonder what might have happened had the defense performed at even an average level. Instead, the Packers managed just an 8-8 record and, after nine seasons, coach Bart Starr was finally fired.

Doug Plank
Safety

His team: Chicago Bears 1975-82
His view: Toughness was the hallmark of a team that was still looking to find itself.

BACK THEN, THEY were still trying to find themselves on offense. There really weren't any great strengths or weaknesses. They weren't really known for being a great running team or a great passing team. There was really nothing you needed to be concerned about. They were just a tough team.

I had a lot of respect for (tight end) Paul Coffman. I really respected him. I never said much to him, but then I didn't say three words to anybody when I played. I think it was a mutual feeling back and forth. But the Packers then just weren't very commanding in any one area, running or passing. But there was also no one over there to really dislike. They just played hard, and I never remember anybody doing anything outside the rules.

Al Baker

Defensive end

His team: Detroit Lions 1978-82; St. *Louis Cardinals 1983-86; Cleveland Browns 1987, 1989-90; Minnesota Vikings 1988 His view: Packers of the 1980s usually counted on their offense first.*

MY ROOKIE YEAR the target was always Lynn Dickey. He wore two knee braces, so we knew if we could get to him, they'd have trouble moving the ball. They weren't the Green Bay Packers of now or the Green Bay Packers of old. They were the Green Bay Packers many people probably wanted to forget.

But I remember in all the times I played against them that I probably didn't see the same (offensive) tackle the entire time I was there. In 1978 I had 23 sacks, and back then (offensive linemen) could still chip block. They can't do that anymore. And the Packers' game plan was always an offensive game plan, and that was not to let Al Baker get started. So they'd do a lot of different things to make sure I didn't.

I remember when Bart Starr was the coach, the offensive policy was three yards and a cloud of dust, and then if you made a mistake on defense, you could go up top and throw it. But once they got behind, they were usually in a lot of trouble.

When we'd play up there, I think the only Lions fans there were us, but we were playing the Green Bay Packers, so that's what made it special.

They were a pocket passing team and I was a pass rusher, and we had five or six guys who could rush the passer, so we usually had pretty good games against them. But we asked ourselves, is that really the way we wanted to treat their quarterback? That's the kind of respect you had for the organization.

They had (running back) Terdell Middleton on a 38 Toss play, or they'd throw it 70 yards to James Lofton. That was about all they had. We knew that going in. But it was always a hard-nosed game. That's the way the division was back then, and Green Bay represented that more than anybody.

There were a few games we could do that in Detroit, but we were a completely different team at home back then. We could actually play football at home.

Doug English

Defensive tackle

His team: Detroit Lions 1975-85
His view: In a division of heated rivals, some of his best friends were Packers players.

EVERY GAME WAS special, and every game was different. Every game gave us certain challenges, and any time we played Green Bay, or even Chicago or Minnesota, it was special. It was the black-and-blue division, and that's what everyone expected.

I liked all those guys on the Packers, because they played the way you were supposed to play. Part of the problem is I had so much respect for the Packers that I don't have any strong memories of any one individual. They just did it the right way.

FACING THE PACKERS AURA

Jeff Siemon

Linebacker

His team: *Minnesota Vikings 1972-82*
His view: *Even in their down years, Packers fans were among the best in the NFL.*

MY ROOKIE SEASON was 1972, and the Packers were a good team, not a great team. I remember they went to the playoffs that year, and they did it with those two great running backs they had: John Brockington and MacArthur Lane. They were almost book-end backs.

Scott Hunter was the quarterback, and he was more a journeyman. He was reliable and steady, but he wasn't going to beat you typically. It was the running game that had to thrive, and it did.

I recall the atmosphere playing in Green Bay, and it was as good an atmosphere as any I recall. The fans were great fans. They were very supportive of their team, but at the same time very respectful of the opposing team. It was a quite a contrast between Green Bay and Chicago. Both were avid fans in many ways, but Green Bay was a great place to play. And if you prevailed against the Packers at Lambeau, there was a measure of respect afforded you by Green Bay fans.

I remember John Brockington very well, because I played against him in the Rose Bowl when I played for Stanford and he played for Ohio State. I was in my junior year, and he was a senior. That was a great Ohio State team with Rex Kern at quarterback and Brockington at running back. It seemed they had All-Americans at every position, but we beat them. It was a huge upset. But I gained a lot of respect for him in that Rose Bowl.

I saw him get drafted by the Packers, and I knew he'd be a great addition. I knew he was a big, tough, hard-running back. He wasn't real big but he was big enough.

That was a pretty good team. Their offensive linemen were always good. Larry McCarren was the center, and he was always a solid player. They were always sound and played mistake-free football.

Doug English

Defensive tackle

His teams: Detroit Lions 1975-85
His view: Some of the best fans in football.

MY FAVORITE GUYS in the league were always Green Bay guys when we went to the Pro Bowl. There were three or four guys that were just cool guys. Those Green Bay guys liked fishing and hunting and being with their families; they were down-to-earth guys.

There's something special about Green Bay and Lambeau Field. The whole time belongs to the team, and there's something interesting about the way of life up there. I guess they're shaped by bitter cold and long winters, but the families all hang together. If mom and dad want to go to the bar, they take their kids with them. They all hang together. It's one of the more family-oriented environments I can recall.

And at the game the fans weren't calling you names. They were backing their team, and that's exactly what they should do. I have an undying respect for the people and the team and the fans.

Doug Plank

Safety

His team: Chicago Bears 1975-82
His view: The fans came from everywhere.

ILOOKED AT THE stadium, and, back then, it wasn't as developed around there then as it is now, and I kept thinking, "Where are all these people coming from?" And the next day there were still motor homes and campers and cars all over the place. Nobody had left. It was stunning. They came from all over the place. They showed up from all over the place.

These guys are all about football and community. You felt like you were in middle America, which, I guess, you were. But I remember at the team hotel down in the restaurant, and having someone serve you that looked just like your grandmother.

For a lot of them it's more than just a football team. It changes your life for a lot of these people. It's such a part of the fabric of life, and I think it always will be.

Joe Theismann

Quarterback

His team: Washington Redskins 1974-85
His view: Packers history still resonates throughout the league.

TODAY, I'M A shareholder in the Green Bay Packers. You're talking about one of the most iconic franchises in professional sports. Mark Murphy (president of the Packers) was one of my teammates, and when they offered up some shares of Packers stock, he suggested I buy some. And what you're doing is basically buying a piece of Americana.

It's one of the great franchises when it comes to understanding the legacy of the game that came before. I mean, you've got Curly Lambeau and Don Hutson and Ray Nitschke and

Bart Starr and Jim Taylor and Paul Hornung. It's all those great players who have been such a big part of the NFL. You could still say those names to anybody, and if they're any kind of a football fan, they know who those players are and what the Green Bay Packers are.

Al Baker

Defensive tackle

His teams: Detroit Lions 1978-82; St. Louis Cardinals 1983-86; Cleveland Browns 1987 , 1989-90; Minnesota Vikings 1988
His view: Packers fans took tailgating to an art form.

I CAN REMEMBER MY feeling as a rookie going to play at Lambeau Field. You're already jittery every single solitary game, but you're especially like that at Lambeau Field. I mean, who didn't love the Packers and respect them?

What was most intimidating to me was that it was this brown bowl, and then I saw the fans. I thought I had seen tailgating before, but then I saw it in Green Bay.

It was all built around the mystique of Lambeau Field, and from what I can see, it's still there. When you go there, you have so much that's going against you. I remember I'd get there three hours before game time, and the parking lot was absolutely jammed. That gets your attention.

And of course there was the weather. Everybody talked about that, especially if you knew you had to play up there at the end of the season.

Later in my career I would up playing for the Minnesota Vikings, and there was a 4 p.m. game and they were still defrosting the field. It was cold but the sun was shining.

I remember the field was all mud, but there were holes in the mud, and one time I sacked the quarterback and I got up and my arms were bleeding from frozen stalactites on the field.

In 1988, when I was with the Vikings, they told me that they didn't wear long sleeves for the cold games in Green Bay. Nobody on the Vikings wore long sleeves. That was the first time I'd ever played in a cold game without wearing long sleeves. They believed it was an advantage, but I'm not so sure about that. They did say bring multiple pairs of shoes, because you had to adjust to the conditions. They had seen Lambeau Field at its worst.

(⬤)

Bob Lurtsema

Defensive end/tackle

His teams: New York Giants 1967-71; Minnesota Vikings 1971-76; Seattle Seahawks 1976-77
His view: Lambeau Field was the best place in the league to play.

I JUST BOUGHT A picture that was signed by Jerry Kramer and Fuzzy Thurston. Both of them are real muddy, and that brought back a lot of memories for me. I just hung that picture up in my garage. There are a lot of great memories.

Lambeau Field is just the greatest. You always rank fields as to what's best and what's worst, and Lambeau was always the best. Philly was the worst. I was a rookie with the New York Giants and I was introduced in a game at Lambeau Field, and the history just exploded in front of my eyes.

And I'd still be playing if we had the benches like they had at Lambeau Field. They were the greatest. There was a shell that covered you, and then there were flaps with hot blowing on your feet. And right where your butt is, there's a warmer, and there were two slots where you can stick your fingers in to keep them warm. It was perfect.

Mark Murphy

Safety

His team: Washington Redskins 1977-84
His view: Corny, and meaningful, that small-market Packers continue to succeed.

GROWING UP, I was aware of the dominant teams Vince Lombardi had. I was very aware of the great history. But I also knew that the Packers had struggled in recent years. In fact, our defensive coordinator with the Redskins, Richie Petitbone, would say to us, "It you don't get better, we'll ship you off to

Green Bay." He used to lump Green Bay in with Buffalo as two places you didn't want to go. They were not a highly regarded team at the time. They had such a long stretch where they struggled.

I remember during the labor negotiations in 1982, I was the Redskins' player representative, and we were making proposals and asking for things. But I remember the owners often used Green Bay as a topic. They'd ask, "How can Green Bay compete?" It was like they needed help from the league.

That's not really the case anymore. There was that renovation in 2003, and we have continued to invest in the stadium. Now I don't think Green Bay's a place too many players don't want to play.

I remember when I was contacted by a search firm about the Packers president position, they asked me if I was interested, and I said "absolutely." I figured I was a long shot for it. But as the process went along, I was fortunate enough to be a finalist and then I got the job. I felt very fortunate because this is such a great organization.

I don't think you can really appreciate it until you're there. In my position, I really have a much better appreciation for the Packers.

And I think it's tremendously meaningful for the league to have a team like Green Bay, and I think it's meaningful in many different ways. We're small market; we have success on the field; and we're able to generate revenue like a larger market. It's corny, but there's something wholesome about a small-market team being able to compete within the big NFL. There's a purity involved with the Packers that's just refreshing. My predecessor (Bob Harlan) called the Packers the greatest story in sports, and I agree with that.

FACING THE PACKERS-BEARS RIVALRY

IN THE LONG, strange, violent history of the National Football League, no two teams are more intricately tied together than the Green Bay Packers and Chicago Bears.

In some ways, they are mirror images of each other, created at the same time by two strong-willed, visionary men who saw what pro football could be, and who were convinced that a professional league was the next logical step.

Contrary to popular belief and NFL lore, the Packers-Bears rivalry is not the longest continuous battle in league history. It just seems that way.

The two teams did not play each other in the strike-shortened season of 1982, but that's just an annoying piece of bookkeeping. And though the two franchises have had their ups and downs over the decades, it remains one of the most heated rivalries in sports.

The team formed by George Halas in Decatur, Illinois, which then after a year was moved to Chicago, first faced the team formed in tiny Green Bay, Wisconsin, by a local sports star, Curly Lambeau, in 1921. Through the 2015 season, they had faced each other 192 times. The Bears won 94, the Packers 92, and there have been six ties. The two teams have only met twice in the playoffs, and they each have won once.

And while it is a series that has seen its share of great players, great games, and unexpected turns, perhaps no period was more memorable and volcanic than a period in the mid-1980s. It was not necessarily great football, because the Bears were clearly ascending and the Packers were still trying to fight their way out of a three-decade struggle.

But while it may not have been great football, it was wonderful theater.

"The rivalry was already set before you got there," said Bears safety Doug Plank, who played from 1975 to 1982. "It was so important to both areas, because you can't have a rivalry if you don't have respect for the other team. And I think we both did. Division titles were important, but in the end it was the rivalry that was most important.

"From 1976 to 1980, it seems like we won every game against them (actually, they won eight of 10), and the one I remember the most was in 1980, when we beat them, 61-7, in Chicago. Bart Starr was still the Packers coach, and that's a game I'll never forget. Everything we did that day went right. But in the years I played, I was on both sides of scores like that. I remember one year we went to Houston and lost, 47-0, and it wasn't even that close. But that's the way it was sometimes. Games like that against the Packers didn't happen very often."

By the end of the 1983 season, though, the relentless mediocrity of Bart Starr's nine seasons as head coach had worn thin, and the beloved former Packers quarterback was finally fired. He was replaced by another Packers legend of the past, Hall of Fame offensive lineman Forrest Gregg, whom Vince Lombardi had once called the best player he had ever coached.

And while Starr was the gentleman head coach who complimented opponents and had his players perform the right way, Gregg brought an edge to his Packers. Meanwhile, another Hall of Famer, former Bears tight end Mike Ditka, took over as Chicago's head coach in 1982 and brought an attitude of his own to his new team.

The results were combustible, and for a three-year period from 1984 to 1986, the two teams engaged in something just short of street warfare.

"It was violent," said Bears defensive tackle Dan Hampton. "Every time out it was violent. But when Forrest Gregg got there, there were a lot of cheap shots. I remember when I retired in 1990, (former Bears linebacker) Ed O'Bradovich talked about playing in the old days against (Packers offensive linemen) Fuzzy Thurston and Jerry Kramer. They were great friends, and I could imagine going out to dinner with those guys. But not then; it was violent. They tried a lot of crap on us."

In that three-year period, as the Bears' prominence grew (including a Super Bowl title in 1985) and the Packers sputtered, the two teams pounded away at each before, during, and after the whistle.

In 1985, while the Bears were marching relentlessly toward the NFL title with a team many observers still believe was the best team in league history, Packers defensive back Ken Still took a fifteen-yard head start and blasted Bears fullback Matt Suhey a good five seconds after the play was over, and as Suhey was merely standing and watching the pile.

It resulted in a penalty on Stills and a rebuke from Ditka, who blamed Gregg for the dirty play.

"The Packers didn't play like that under Bart," Ditka said after the game.

For his part, Gregg complimented Stills for the aggressive play.

"I wish I had twenty guys like him," Gregg was quoted as saying afterward.

But the bad blood reached its peak the following season, when Packers defensive end Charles Martin came onto Lambeau Field for a November game with a towel listing the names of Bears players he wanted to take out of the game. One was quarterback Jim McMahon.

He got his chance later in the game after McMahon threw an interception. In a play still burned into the memories of Bears and Packers players and fans alike, Martin tracked down McMahon from behind, lifted him up by the waist and threw him to the ground, separating McMahon's shoulder. The injury ended McMahon's season and all but derailed the Bears' hopes for a second straight Super Bowl title.

After the game, Packers linebacker Brian Noble found Suhey and said simply, "This has got to stop."

It did, eventually, when Gregg quit after the 1987 season to coach his alma mater, SMU.

Since then, the rivalry has burned as hot as ever but has not reached the level of hostility it did in the mid-1980s.

"I really respect the Packers now," Hampton said. "They do it the right way, but it's still a great rivalry."

Doug Plank

Safety

His team: Chicago Bears 1975-82
His view: The Bears-Packers rivalry remains the essence of what the NFL is supposed to be.

I THINK BOTH THE Bears and Packers were such iconic members of the NFL from the beginning. There were so many Hall of Famers and stars, the tradition was already set. The rivalry between the two was already set before you got there. It was so important to people in both areas, because you can't have a rivalry if you don't have the respect. So many have thought it was important in terms of winning the division, but it's the rivalry that was important. The burden has always been on both teams. For me, the rivalry overrode everything.

Players always try saying it's just another game, but the fans will never let you see that, because it's not that way with the fans. How do you not have competition when you have two teams that are so close to each other? I truly believe in my heart that, if they're not playing each other, people in the rivalry are rooting for the other team. If I wasn't playing against the Packers, I'd be rooting for them, and I still do that.

That rivalry really went deep. I remember one year, in 1975 or '76, it was the end of the season, and we were playing up in Green Bay. It was freezing cold. I couldn't believe how cold it was. The Packers said there were heaters on our sidelines, but I didn't feel any heaters.

Anyway, one of our safeties was hurt during the game, and we had a young guy who didn't want to come off the bench and go into the game. So Mike Adamle said he'd go in. Now Mike Adamle was a running back. That shows you how crazy the league was back then. So Mike plays two plays at safety, because the other guy wouldn't get out there. But it was a chance to get on the field against the Packers.

And, yes, it did get dirty for a time, but nothing like it did in the mid-'80s. I was gone before all that really started.

But when you have guys like Forrest Gregg coaching against Mike Ditka, you know something is bound to happen. You had two boiling pots of water, and they reflected that to their teams. Players like to take on the personalities of their coach, and that was certainly the case in Green Bay with Forrest Gregg and in Chicago with Ditka. You knew something was going to happen. I'm not saying that Bart Starr (who coached the Packers for nine seasons before being fired and replaced by Gregg) wasn't emotional, but he wasn't as quick to anger.

And that was standard operating procedure. If someone did something to your teammate, you went back into the huddle and said that we were going to even the score. Back then, no one was going to kick you out of the game. Now teams are sending film back to the league (for possible fines). But back then, football was not played frame by frame. It was intimidation. So much of that is built into the rules, but the goal is to beat the other team into submission.

That was the great thing about that rivalry. Everybody played hard.

Jim Osbourne

Defensive tackle

His team: Chicago Bears 1972-84

His view: Playing the Packers was always a good, clean dogfight.

WHEN I THINK of playing the Packers, regardless of what our record was or what their record was, it was always a dogfight. It was a good, clean dogfight, and you knew going into the game that you were going to put forth all the effort you could, because you knew they were going to do the same thing.

I remember there were a couple of my college teammates on the Packers, and we knew we'd get together after the game and we'd laugh about it. But during the game it was all business. It was good clean fun where you went all out, and afterward you left it on the field. That was the way to play.

I remember that game in 1980, when the Packers beat us in overtime. That was really something.

(Author's note: In the season opener at Lambeau Field, the Packers and Bears were tied at 6-6 and went into overtime, when Green Bay kicker Chester Marcol lined up for a 35-yard field goal. The kick was blocked, but the ball bounced right back to the tiny, bespectacled Marcol, who instinctively grabbed the ball and ran around left end for a 25-yard game-winning touchdown. Mobbed in the end zone by jubilant teammates, Marcol collapsed in tears and was nearly carried off the field by teammates. Meanwhile, Bears players stood by with hands on their hips, still unsure what had transpired.)

Oh yeah, I was on the field for that one. I was in the middle of the line along with Alan Page. He'd had a great career with the Vikings and was finishing his career with the Bears. He was my roommate that year. He had it down to almost a science on how to block field goals.

Our plan was always to try to move the center back, so both he and I would line up over the center, and it was my job to drive the center back. Then he'd put his hands up at just the right time. He'd blocked quite a few field goals over the years.

So the ball is snapped and I'm driving the center, and I got a really good push on the center. I'm buried under a pile, but I hear a thud and I knew Alan had blocked it. I'm still under the pile, but then I hear the crowd go crazy, and I knew the crowd wasn't cheering for us. I didn't know what happened until I got home and saw the replay. It was the craziest thing I'd ever seen.

I remember a lot about Chester Marcol. What I remember early on is that Chester would invariably kick the winning field goal against us. You'd be fighting hard the whole game, and then he'd come in and kick a winning field goal. That was awfully frustrating.

I remember one game, I can't remember the year, but Abe Gibron was our coach (he was the Bears head coach from 1972 to 1974), and Marcol kicked a field goal. Gibron told us on the sideline before the next kickoff that he wanted one guy deep to catch the ball, and he wanted everyone else to go after Chester Marcol. So he kicks off and he looks down and sees what's going on, and his eyes get really wide. So instead of running down-field, he makes a beeline for the sidelines. One of the funniest things I've ever seen. But that was the Bears-Packers rivalry. Nothing was off limits.

Tom Hicks

Linebacker

His team: Chicago Bears 1976-80
His view: Something strange always happened when the Bears
and Packers played.

YEAH, I WAS on the field for that, too. I was the wing
guy on both extra points and field goals. I couldn't believe
what I was seeing.

It ended up being kind of a sweep play. The ball landed in his
(Marcol's) arms, and he just started running. Chester was not
fast but no one was there, so no one was going to get to him. I
saw what was happening and—what's the phrase now?—it was
like, "You've got to be kidding me."

But I think one of the more memorable aspects of that play
was that we had a guy on the sidelines, Jerry Meyers, who was
so mad at what happened he jumped up and tore up his knee.
He was that mad.

But that was part of the rivalry. And it was a good one.
Personally, for me, rivalries come out of the individual battles
and philosophies.

When Forrest Gregg was coach, the Packers were just so
dirty. They were very dirty, and when you played someone
like that it really gets you going. Maybe it was left over from

when there were eight teams in the original NFL, or something like that. Maybe it was from when teams would take trains to games. I don't know. But back then they were jobs, and it was their job to get those frustrations out. But team versus team rivalries? I think that's more for the press and fans. I think that was more of a media creation.

It's great for sports. It's a lot of fun. But for players, it's more about individual or philosophy-based. When I played, Bart Starr was the Packers coach, and Walter (Payton, the Bears' all-time leading rusher) was in the early part of his career. But even though it was such a great rivalry, I remember Packers fans would applaud for the Bears' Walter when he had a good game. They recognized how special he was, and that response was pretty remarkable.

But speaking of individual rivalries, I had a pretty good one with Larry McCarren. He was Green Bay's center and a very good player. He was a (University of Illinois) graduate like me, but he was a senior at Illinois when I was a sophomore or freshman. I went through training camp with him, and he was always good to me.

He didn't talk much, but then we both get to the NFL and I'm a middle linebacker and he's a center, so we faced each other a lot. I'll say this, he was one of the better holders I've played against. And during a game I'm on the referee telling him to get Larry off me. I'd yell at him to stop holding, but Larry would just look at me and smile. Man-on-man I was outmatched, and I knew it. He was a better player than I was.

Tom Thayer

Offensive tackle

His team: Chicago Bears 1985-92; Miami Dolphins 1993
His view: *"Replay game" is the one that will always stay with me.*

I GREW UP IN Joliet, Illinois, so you always knew as a Bears fan all about the rivalry with the Packers. Everyone knew a lot about it. When I started playing for the Bears, (head coach Mike) Ditka made mention of it enough. He talked every year about beating the Packers. No matter what the records were, they'd always be hard-fought games, and the Packers game always had more meaning than other games.

The game I remember most is the only one I lost at Lambeau. That was the Don Majkowski game (in 1989). That one is still unbelievable to me.

(Author's note: In one of the most dramatic games in the rivalry's long and already dramatic history, the Packers beat the Bears with thirty-five seconds to play, when quarterback Don Majkowski threw a 14-yard touchdown pass to Sterling Sharpe that at first was declared a touchdown, then flagged as a penalty when Majkowski was ruled to have thrown the ball after crossing the line of scrimmage. But a new replay system, installed just that season, reviewed the play and ruled, after a nearly three-minute delay, that Majkowski had not crossed the line. The Lambeau Feld crowd erupted, and the Packers won the game, 14-13. To this day, Bears fans and players alike insist Majkowski's throw was illegal, and, even today, Packers revel in telling the Bears that, "After further review, the Bears still suck.")

I just remember how mad Ditka was in the locker room after the game. And it wasn't so much about the call. It was about losing to the Packers. That started the ball rolling downhill. He was so angry it continued to the next day when we had our film review session. Ditka would never let you feel you lost the game on one play. It was a culmination of plays, and he believed that one play never cost you a game. It was a lot of plays and a lot of mistakes that made that last play so important. He hated that. So that was a really bad film session. You had to have a thick skin when he evaluated you.

But losing to the Packers was especially tough for Ditka. With Ditka's years of professional football, the Bears just couldn't lose to the Packers. The records never really mattered; you just had to beat the Packers.

Steve McMichael
Defensive tackle/Nose tackle

His teams: New England Patriots 1980; Chicago Bears 1981-93; Green Bay Packers 1994
His view: The Packers' cheap shots told us that we had arrived as a team.

THAT WAS PROBABLY the biggest compliment. I thought it was an insult when it was going on, but it turned out to be a compliment. You know what it was? They started cheap-shotting us. They'd knock (star running back) Walter Payton over the bench. There was (defensive end) Charles Martin cheap-shotting (quarterback) Jim McMahon. He threw him down and separated his shoulder (in 1986), and that pretty much ended his career as a starting quarterback.

That told me how good we were, because that's the way inferior teams had to play. That was the Packers admitting to me that *we're* more than *you* are, so that's how we have to play.

But I remember how much the populace of Green Bay was so offended at how we dominated the series back then.

I loved playing against the Packers in Lambeau. Until they built that underground tunnel, we had to walk through the bowels of the stadium and through a chain link fence. There were fans on both sides of us, and they're throwing beer on you and cursing you. It was great. After the game you'd smell like beer, but we knew we were only as great as our greatest opponent, and that's what fueled the Packers' need to keep resorting to cheap shots.

I remember in 1985, the second game we played them that season, and it was at Lambeau. The guys who got there early went into the locker room, and there was like a hundred pounds of horse (crap) on the locker room floor. Don't tell me about Lambeau Field security. They got it out of there before the other guys got there, but that really got our attention.

Then we look outside and see a bunch of Packers with sledgehammers beating on a refrigerator with the No. 72 on it (referring to the Bears' 375-pound nose tackle William "Refrigerator" Perry). I knew then I wasn't in Kansas anymore, Dorothy.

In those years, we kind of dominated the Packers (from 1985 to 1988 the Bears won eight straight). They'd win one every once in a while, but every now and then a blind squirrel will find an acorn. One of those came in 1989, when Don Majkowski threw a pass over the line of scrimmage and beat us. He knows he was over the line. We see each other every one in a while, and he still tells me that. But I think I even shook their hands after that game. It happens.

Dan Hampton

Defensive tackle

His team: Chicago Bears 1979-90
His view: The importance of the Packers-Bears rivalry was made clear very early on.

I GOT TO THE Bears in 1979, and it just so happened that coming out of the University of Arkansas, I never had any wish to play for the Chicago Bears. I wanted to go to Miami or Los Angeles, somewhere by the ocean. I didn't understand the profound place I had now been put in. In the world of pro football there is Mecca, and that's Green Bay and Chicago.

The oldest rivalry in football was the Chicago Bears against the Green Bay Packers, and I didn't understand this at the time. And in all the years I played, and it's been 37 or 38 years I've been involved in football, I still didn't understand it.

I knew about the Ice Bowl, those were legendary talks, but I really didn't comprehend what it all meant. I do remember my very first game in the NFL was in Chicago, and we beat the Packers, 6-3, on a really hot day. The next year we opened in Green Bay, and that was that blocked Chester Marcol field goal that he ran in for a touchdown. It was crazy. But it was always a good game with them. It was violent. They played hard against us.

It had always been a good, clean, tough rivalry with the Packers when Bart was head coach, but in the mid-1980s, when Forrest Gregg took over as head coach, there were a lot of cheap shots, and we got into a pretty heated rivalry with the Packers.

It might have had something to do with the fact that, for the first three or four years of my career, the Packers were relatively even with us. After that, we began to dominate them. We just had better players. I remember that Monday night game in 1985 when the Fridge (380-pound nose tackle William Perry) ran over their linebacker (George Cumby). For years and years we always wanted to compete against the Packers, but that game we almost seemed like we broke their will. We knew it, and so did they.

They tried all kinds of crap with us, and we had to basically even the score, so to speak. We tried to pillage as much as we could. Rivalries are what they are.

But today I really respect the Packers. It's a different type of organization, and it means so much to the people of Wisconsin. I respect the fact that they were one of the first franchises that "got it." They knew the right way to get the job done, and I credit (former team president) Bob Harlan with that. He brought in the right people, and that's turned them into a perennial winner.

But it's still a great rivalry. It's been frustrating being a Bears fans and watching how the Packers have dominated them over the years. And those quarterbacks they've had. Are you kidding me? They go from one Hall of Famer in Brett Favre, and now they've got Aaron Rodgers, who will probably be a Hall of Famer, too. They've done such a good job in that regard. It's gone from hatred of the Packers in the 1980s to a grudging respect. You respect them because they do it the right way, and they're always so well prepared.

Extra Point

"It Was a Spectacle"

Next to the Ice Bowl, it may be the most talked-about game in the Packers' long, storied, sometimes bizarre history.

The game played October 17, 1983, between the Packers and the powerful Washington Redskins in front of a thoroughly enthralled national TV audience on Monday night at Lambeau Field clearly falls into that category. It was a game no one expected, and one which few, even today, can explain.

"I'll never forget that Monday night game we played against them in 1983," former Washington Redskins quarterback Joe Theismann recalled. "What a night."

It was all that and maybe a little bit more.

The setup, in retrospect, was ideal for what would eventually unveil itself before a full house at Lambeau.

The Redskins, fresh off winning the Super Bowel the season before, were, in no uncertain terms, an offensive juggernaut.

"In 1983 it was never a question of if we'd win or lose," Theismann said. "It was how many points we'd score. That's just who we were. With the style of offense we had with three tight ends, we'd go to three wide receivers, and then we'd create mismatches."

The Redskins' offense featured bruising veteran running back John Riggins, and they'd alter the scheme with fast, elusive Joe Washington, who could not only run but was a terrific receiver. There were tight ends Clint Didier, Don Warren, and Rick Walker, and a fleet of receivers including Art Monk, Charlie Brown, and Alvin Garrett. And it was all triggered by Theismann, the NFL's MVP that season, who was having the best season of his career.

The Redskins would go on to score 541 points that season, which was an NFL record at the time, and reach their second straight Super Bowl, where they were beaten by the Los Angeles Raiders.

The Packers of 1983? Well . . . not so much.

Bart Starr's unit on offense could almost match the Redskins in firepower, as it featured quarterback Lynn Dickey, wide receiver James Lofton, and tight end Paul Coffman. Those Packers would go on to score a not-unimpressive 429 points of their own as they posted an 8-8 record.

The issue was the defense, which couldn't stop anyone. Indeed, the Packers allowed a staggering 6,403 yards that season, the most in the NFL, as well as 28 rushing touchdowns, also an NFL worst. Through some statistical anomaly, however, the Packers were only the 26th worst defense in the league behind the Houston Oilers and San Diego Chargers, and the 439 points they allowed also trailed only the Oilers and Chargers.

So Washington rolled into Green Bay that October night full of confidence. They had just come off an impressive win over the St. Louis Cardinals the Sunday before to move to 5-1. The Packers had been blasted by the Detroit Lions the previous week and were an ordinary 3-3.

And while Theismann claimed the Redskins were not overconfident heading into the game, several Packers claimed otherwise.

"I think they thought they were going to come and roll over us," said Dickey, who could tell in pregame warmups that something was different at his end, as well. "The ball was coming out of my hand so well. It felt great."

Theismann said he felt the same way.

"I did feel that way," he said. "It sort of felt like that all year for me. I felt I could put the ball exactly where I wanted to."

Redskins safety Mark Murphy remembers the game was a blur of big plays and seemingly nonstop touchdowns.

"I think we were confident," said Murphy, who is now president of the Packers. "We were playing as well as anybody in the league, but we ran into a buzzsaw. Especially with the Packers offense. I played a lot of games in my career, and it was the wildest game I was ever a part of. It was like a Ping-Pong match. It was definitely not a good game to be a defensive player."

Over the course of the next three-plus hours, the Packers and Redskins slammed at each other in an offensive orgy that left NFL fans talking for years.

"I remember the atmosphere—it was electric," Murphy said. "It was a big deal to play on Monday night back then, and the Packers didn't play a lot of national TV games. This was a big deal for Green Bay, and I still hear about that all the time. It was a very much like a college game in terms of how much the fans were into the game. It was a just a great game."

"You were playing at Lambeau Field so you weren't going to run over anybody, but every time we touched the ball, we seemed to score," Theismann said.

Then again, so did the Packers.

"We would score a touchdown, and I'd come to the sideline and go through my routine," Theismann said. "I'd sit down, fold a towel. But every time I tried that in that game, I'd never get a chance because (left guard) Russ Grimm would come over and say, 'They scored again. Let's go.' It was really something."

Murphy, too, remembers how both offenses simply roared past opposing defenses like they were standing still.

"You think of the receivers the Packers had," he said. "They had James Lofton and John Jefferson, and Paul Coffman was a great tight end. And Lynn Dickey was a great quarterback. Both defenses were back on their heels the whole game. It was a bad game to be a defender, a bad game to be a defensive back and a bad game to be a defensive back named Mark Murphy."

Ironically, the Packers did indeed have a safety of their own named Mark Murphy.

In the end, after a Jan Stenerud twenty-yard goal with 50 seconds left to play gave the Packers a 48-47 lead, the Redskins had a final chance to win.

"That last drive (which went 55 yards in six plays with no timeouts) was probably the best of my career," Theismann said. "We kept throwing wide to Joe Washington, and I remember at the end I told Charlie Brown in the huddle, I said, 'I'm not going to look at you, but I need about 15 yards and I'm going throw you the ball.' I executed it the way I wanted to."

That set up the potential game-winning 39-yard field goal attempt by veteran Mark Moseley. But in a game that produced a total of 1,025 yards of offense, it came down to a rushed field-goal attempt that Moseley missed to the right, giving the Packers the improbable victory.

Even all these year later, Theismann, who was the holder for field-goal attempts, recalls the aftermath.

"I looked at him and said, 'You've got to be kidding me,'" Theismann said. "His response was, 'You missed the mark (on the field)' Remember that Mark was one of the last straight-on kickers, and his margin for error was a lot smaller than it is for sidewinders."

Maybe that's the only way a game like this could have ended.

Dickey completed 22 of 31 passes for 387 yards and three touchdowns. Coffman caught six passes for 124 yards and two scores, while Gerry Ellis added four receptions for 105 yards, and James Lofton added five catches for 96 yards.

On the Redskins' side, Theismann completed 27 of 39 passes for 398 yards and two scores, both to Joe Washington. The Packers gained a total of 552 yards, and the Packers rung up 473 total yards.

"It was a dream game for a quarterback, because you knew you couldn't hand the ball off, because if you're always down seven points, a game like that you know you're going to be down 14," Theismann said. "What was surprising to me about that game was our defense, and how well Green Bay was able to move the ball against our defense. You look at it and say, how do you give up 48 points? And I remember after that game, we always made Mark kick a 39-yard field goal in practice. He was never going to miss a 39-yard field goal again. He kicked and kicked and kicked."

He laughs about it even now.

"That game was a spectacle," he said. "And every year I still get my picture taken with James Lofton."

Murphy laughs, too.

"I've gotten to know James Lofton pretty well over the years, and he's said to me, 'Mark, I never got hit harder than when you hit me in that game,'" Murphy said. "And I said, 'Really? I don't remember anything good from that game.'"

CHAPTER 3

RETURN TO TITLETOWN

AS ANOTHER LOST season was coming to a depressing close, Green Bay Packers president Bob Harlan had finally had enough.

The team he had devoted his career to, the team that he had joined as a public relations assistant twenty years earlier, was going nowhere way too fast for his own good, and change, real change, was needed.

It had been twenty-five years since the proud Packers organization had known anything like real success. They had reached the playoffs only twice since Vince Lombardi quit as head coach after the 1967 season. In that time, five coaches, including two former Packers icons in Bart Starr and Forrest Gregg, had failed to change the dynamic.

In those twenty-four seasons since Lombardi stepped down, the Packers had known five winning seasons and just two playoff berths. That was bad enough, Harlan knew, but now the organization was sliding toward something close to irrelevance, and the time had come for major, seismic change.

So, late in the 1991 season, as the Packers were hurtling toward a 4-12 finish under fourth-year head coach Lindy Infante, Harlan made the decision that would change everything.

He contacted a man he had admired for years, Ron Wolf, a consummate football guy who had come up through the ranks with the Oakland Raiders and then the New York Jets, and asked him if he was interested in taking over the steaming wreckage that was the Packers.

"Everybody told me I was crazy to even consider it," Wolf recalls.

Harlan's offer was simple but overwhelming: He would wield the kind of power as general manager that had not been seen in Green Bay since Lombardi cast his massive shadow over everything. He could hire coaches and run the draft, and make the changes that needed to be made. Harlan only wanted one thing in return: make the Packers a force again.

Wolf admitted years later that he had his doubts initially. But he was also intrigued by the opportunity to rebuild a franchise, essentially from the ground up.

So he accepted Harlan's charge, and he wasted no time in doing two things: checking out an overweight, unruly, undisciplined number three quarterback languishing on the Atlanta Falcons bench, and firing Infante after the season finale.

Those two decisions would also go hand-in-hand in terms of the future of the Packers.

For Wolf, who knew his first hire as head coach had to be a home run, really had only two names on his list: the veteran Bill Parcells and an up-and-coming offensive coordinator from the San Francisco 49ers, Mike Holmgren.

Parcells, a long-time friend of Wolf's, wanted more decision-making power than the new GM was willing to give him. Besides, he'd already spoken with Holmgren and knew he was the guy the Packers needed.

Unfortunately, so did several other franchises.

The Minnesota Vikings, Tampa Bay Buccaneers, Pittsburgh Steelers, and Los Angeles Rams, among others, were also seeking new coaches, and Holmgren, by far, was the NFL's hottest head coaching prospect.

At the same time, Wolf had been keeping his eye on that quarterback in Atlanta, Brett Favre, whom Falcons coach Jerry Glanville had not-so-kiddingly called the "Pillsbury Doughboy."

Favre, with a breathtakingly strong arm but little work ethic, was miserable in Atlanta and knew that the only way he'd play, according to Glanville, was if the rest of the entire Falcons team was killed in a plane crash.

But Wolf had been enamored with Favre from the days when Favre had played for Southern Mississippi. He saw greatness in all the ragged edges and felt he was a quarterback to build a team around.

So the two pieces were coming together.

Intrigued by Wolf and the direction he had charted for the team, Holmgren agreed in January 1992 to take over as Green Bay's head coach, and, not even a month later, Wolf traded his number one draft pick to the Falcons for Favre.

To Wolf, two massive pieces of a successful rebuild were in place: a coach and a quarterback. Now came the really hard part, making those head-strong pieces work together while finding the other part of the puzzle.

FACING THE PACKERS AURA

Paul Gruber

Left tackle

Hs team: Tampa Bay Buccaneers 1988-99
His view: Having grown up in Wisconsin, it was always special playing at Lambeau Field.

IT'S FUNNY. I grew up in Wisconsin, and, to be honest, when I was growing up the Packers stunk. I grew up in Madison (and played for the University of Wisconsin), so their games were blacked out (on TV) when they played in Milwaukee. That was my memory as a young kid. I never remembered the glory days.

I remember when Bart Starr was the coach, and then Forrest Gregg coached, but they just weren't very good. Everyone in Wisconsin was a Packers fan, and everyone said they were die-hard fans, but I'm not sure if that was true. If I had a favorite team as a kid it was probably the Denver Broncos, and then in high school and college it was the Chicago Bears, because they trained not too far away in Platteville. And I liked the way they played.

But I would have loved to have played for the Packers, regardless of their history. I remember I was pretty confident I'd be a top 10 draft coming out of college. You kind of knew there were a few teams that needed a left tackle, but the Packers weren't one of them. They had Ken Ruettgers, so I realized pretty quickly that wasn't going to happen.

When I got to play at Lambeau Field, though, I remember how special it was. Being from Wisconsin, I was able to play in front of friends and family, and to be in Green Bay in general and Lambeau Field in particular, it's one of those iconic stadiums. It's like going to some sort of chapel of football. It's awesome to be able to play in that environment.

Don Beebe

Wide receiver

His teams: Buffalo Bills 1989-94; Carolina Panthers 1995; Green Bay Packers 1996-97
His view: Green Bay remains a unique experience for the entire NFL.

I **GREW UP IN** the Chicago area, so I was a Bears fan. My dad and I would sit down and watch games all the time, and we all knew the history of the Bears-Packers rivalry. I knew it very well, going back to the Lombardi-Halas days.

But I remember when I was in Buffalo with James Lofton. He had played for the Packers, and he said to me one day, "Beebs, if you ever get a chance to play in Green Bay and at Lambeau Field you ought to do it." He said, "First and foremost, it's Lambeau Field. You think of all the history there." He talked about how it was a community-owned team and how great the field itself was. He said, "It's an amazing field. It's fast, the grass is cut short, and you can run there. You've got to experience it." And, lo and behold, I did.

The first experience I had was when I joined the Packers in 1996, and we had a preseason scrimmage and there were 60,000 people watching. I mean, it was a scrimmage. That was overwhelming to me. It was so unique. And everything that went with it, like riding a kid's bike every day in training camp from the locker room to the practice field. You just felt part of the community. It was just one big family.

I'm a small-town guy myself, and I didn't want to sign with the New York Jets or another big city team. Green Bay was closer to home. My biggest factor was, I wanted to go to a team with a chance to win the Super Bowl. The Packers were one of four or five teams at that time with that chance. I was right.

I think the biggest difference between the Buffalo Bills and the Packers in the Super Bowl was that the Bills just couldn't handle the emotion of the game.

The best example was Super Bowl XXVIII against the Cowboys in Atlanta. We're winning at halftime. We're handling them. After three times to the Super Bowl we're going to win this, and we felt really good coming out after halftime. But on the third or fourth play from scrimmage, Thurman Thomas fumbles and (the Cowboys') James Washington runs it back in for a touchdown. Now we still had a whole second half to play, but it was dead silence on our sideline. We were deer in headlights, and we ended up losing.

Now it's Super XXXI and I'm with the Packers, and we're playing the Patriots. We went up 10-0, but Drew Bledsoe throws a touchdown pass, and we're down, 14-10. I came to the sideline after that, and with the leaders of the team it was completely different. They said, "We're fine. This is no different than the rest of the season." It's the team that handles the emotion of the game. You had to stay positive, and that's what we did.

Then I went to my sixth Super Bowl the next season and we lost, but that bothers me for a different reason. That was the hardest one for me. I had battled injuries that whole season, and I had kind of tweaked my hamstring late in the season. But I told Mike (Holmgren) I'd be ready for the Super Bowl, and, sure enough, I practiced that whole week in Green Bay, and we go to San Diego and I practiced that Monday before the game.

Tuesday was media day, and then on Wednesday Mike calls me down to his hotel room and told me he wasn't going to dress me for the game. It came out of left field. I said, "Mike, this ain't gonna work. I'm ready to play." Now I love Mike and there are no hard feelings, but that really hurt. He said there was a wide receiver, Ronnie Anderson, who had been on the practice squad, and they didn't want to lose him to free agency, so they were going to dress him instead. I think it was two or three weeks after the Super Bowl, and they cut him.

The hardest part was, I went back to my room after he told me, and I was devastated. Bill Schroeder was my roommate, and I went back to my room and I cried my eyes out. But how we lost that game was the toughest part, because I know I could have helped them win. If I'd had a different personality, I probably would have said something. But I wasn't going to say anything. That's not my style.

Mike Alstott

Fullback

His team: Tampa Bay Buccaneers 1996-2006
His view: The Packers helped us become a team to contend with.

GROWING UP IN Chicago, I had a lot of memories of the Bears and Packers. It was an unbelievable rivalry. Then when I got into the league, in the mid- to late-'90s, I had a chance to go against guys like Brett Favre and Reggie White, and all the other great players: that was pretty impressive for me.

I was more of a Redskins fan growing up, but I watched the Bears all the time. When I got to the Bucs, being able to establish our own rivalry with the Packers was important. And that individual rivalry between Brett and (Bucs defensive tackle) Warren Sapp was really important. It gave us an identity.

At the same time, it was important for me to go to Lambeau Field. I mean, Lambeau was Lambeau. Everybody knew about it, and you always knew or heard about it. I finally had a chance as an opponent to play there. It was a special place to play. I believe we went to the '97 playoffs and played up there. That was a very cool place to play. We came up short, but what a great experience for a young team.

It was a fight every time we played those guys, especially after we established ourselves. But we learned against a great team, and it made us better.

And I'll always remember Packers fans. It's a great fan base, and it was always such a great atmosphere to play there. We'd come over on the bus on game day and go through those neighborhoods, and then you'd see Lambeau Field rise up. That really impressed a lot of the new guys when they first saw that. And you see those neighborhoods where people charged $20 to park on the front lawns of their homes. Everybody was making money off their lawns. I thought that was pretty cool.

And Packers fans were everywhere. I remember my first game ever in the "Old Sombrero" (Tampa Stadium) in 1996, and we opened the season against the Packers. We hadn't established ourselves yet, and the crowd was a sea of yellow and green. A lot of us were really surprised, but that's when we knew we had to establish ourselves as a team.

Tim Krumrie

Nose tackle

His team: Cincinnati Bengals 1983-94
His view: I always wanted to play for the Green Bay Packers.

I GREW UP IN a little farm town in Wisconsin (Mondovi), and I watched all their games on TV as a kid. Then I went to the University of Wisconsin, so I became a Packers fan immediately. I ended up playing in the NFL for the Cincinnati Bengals, and you're playing the Packers. And for a Wisconsin kid, you just can't imagine when you're playing there in Lambeau Field.

What I remember is the intensity of playing there. Oh my God, that's what you remember. Coming from Wisconsin and growing up there, it was nice.

And I also learned that the Packers name is carried across the world. When I travel, I have a Wisconsin hat on, and people will say "Are you a Packers fan?" It's kind of a joke. They'll say, "Where are you from?" and when you tell them Wisconsin, they'll always say, "Ah, Green Bay Packers." It's really amazing, but that's just the reputation the Packers have, no matter where you go.

You just love the Green Bay Packers, and all the wins they had and all the championships. It's just a special place. When you go into that stadium, you learn fast that you better watch out. It's a matter of look out or get out.

I wanted to be a Packer, and I wanted fans cheering for me. We had great fans in Cincinnati, and they always supported us. But there was always something different about Packers fans. It always seemed they were actually out there on the field with the team.

(HHHHH)

Gary Plummer

Linebacker

His teams: San Diego Chargers 1986-93; San Francisco 49ers 1994-97

His view: Playing football at Lambeau Field was a pure football experience.

THE FIRST THING that really struck me was that I was a Packers fan as a six- or seven-year-old kid, because I saw the first two Super Bowls, and the Packers won them both.

But it wasn't until my twelfth year in the NFL, when I was playing for the 49ers, that I finally played in Lambeau Field. It was amazing that I'd been in the league that long and never played there. I remember it was a great game. It was a Monday Night game (in 1996), and the Packers won it in overtime.

But what really struck me was when I did my postgame TV show. I had a show I did after every game, so I was out on the field and already dressed. It was a good thirty minutes after the game, and there were still 35,000 people in the stands. The University of Wisconsin band was playing polka songs, and it reminded me of a college football game; that's how pure it was.

I'd played in Kansas City, where the fans threw snowballs at you, and in Oakland they threw batteries at you. But people in Green Bay are coming by and saying, "Hey Plummer, you played a great game, and we'll see you in the playoffs." I didn't even know that they knew who I was. It was shocking. Everyone was so positive.

If you're in New York, it's, "We kicked your ass. You suck." But in Green Bay, it was a wonderful experience. That really exceeded my expectations.

You can also see what an amazing home-field advantage the Packers had, and still have. You can have some idea what it means, but until you experience it, you don't really know the intensity.

Vince Workman
Running back

His teams: Green Bay Packers 1989-92; Tampa Bay Buccaneers 1993-94; Carolina Panthers 1995; Indianapolis Colts 1995-96
His view: It was a strange, wonderful experience going back to play against the Packers.

PLAYING AGAINST MY former teammates, it was very emotional. I did not leave Green Bay on bad terms. Ron Wolf had brought in another running back, John Stephens, to be the featured back, and the writing was kind of on the wall for me to leave.

I went to Tampa Bay, and the biggest reason was to play for my former running backs coach who had been in Green Bay, Willie Peete. I was very excited to play against the Packers that first time in 1993.

I remember I went to dinner the night before the game with my friend Darrell Thompson, who was still a running back with the Packers. We each decided to reveal one secret we knew the other team would do the next day. We were both on offense, so it wouldn't impact the game. It ended up being a trick play each offense was going to run. We both used them, too, but the Packers executed theirs a little bit better than we did.

When we went back to play the Packers later in the season in Green Bay, I was the starting tailback, and it was a little bit different because it was Lambeau Field. I was going to go back to Lambeau, and it was such a special place. It was good to be back there. I remember I was on the team bus, and Packers fans would cheer my name. There was never anything negative. Before the game, I remember I needed a pair of gloves, because it was colder than I expected. So I went over to the Packers locker room, and (Packers equipment manager) Red Batty gave me a pair. Just like that.

I can honestly say that playing in different places around the league, from my experience, Packers fans were easily the best. My nickname ("Pookie") was well known to Packers fans, and I saw a sign in the stands that said "We Miss You Pookie." That was heartwarming. I remember I had one of my best games as a Buccaneer that day, but we still lost. But it was a fun game to play in. They were my brothers.

After that game, Brett (Favre) came up to me and we talked, and he said, "Pookie, we miss you." I wanted to come back. I wish I'd never left.

I tell people all the time that there are certain places in the world you ought to go and experience, and one of them is a Packers game at Lambeau Field. Everyone should go one time, because it's that special. There's just something about the whole area, the town. The state of Wisconsin embraces that team; it goes way back. You're talking about almost one hundred years of history with the Packers. It's hard to explain. You have to experience it to understand it.

113

Max Lane
Offensive tackle/guard

His team: New England Patriots 1994-2000
His view: It was a surreal experience playing in Green Bay for the first time.

WE PLAYED GREEN Bay several times in the preseason, because (head coach) Bill Parcells always liked to play NFC teams a lot in the preseason. He thought it was a good way for us to play against teams from the other conference, to get us ready for the regular season.

I remember it was my rookie year and we played Green Bay in our last preseason game, and I had a chance to go up against (Packers defensive end) Reggie White. Of course, he wasn't nearly at the top of his game in the preseason.

But it was pretty surreal from the point of landing at the airport and going to the hotel. This was Green Bay, so it was pretty special. We didn't go to the stadium the day before the game, since it was a preseason game and we were playing at night. So we took the bus to the game, and it felt like we were going to a big high school game. We were going through these neighborhoods, and then all of a sudden up pops this stadium, almost out of nowhere. And with me being a rookie, it was all pretty new to me. I mean, I came from this little town in Missouri, so this was really something.

My dad was a big Green Bay Packers fan. He was born in the '30s, and he followed the Packers in the '60s, when it was their heyday. He always talked about how he loved the Packers, so playing them was pretty neat. I remember I called my dad after the game, and he was excited to hear about Lambeau Field and that I'd played there.

I know when the Packers won the Super Bowl in '96, it was pretty special to a lot of people. I wish it hadn't come against us, but I remember how many people were happy about it. There had been a pretty big gap between the Packers of the '60s and that point. There had been a lot of down years, so this was a real resurrection for them. The mystique had returned; that's what was said back then. I think it was a little overblown, but is there a team like that nowadays? The only team I know of is the Packers. No team really does it the way they do.

Thirty years from now, people will look back at what they did. The 1980s was the decade of the 49ers, and in the 1970s it was the Pittsburgh Steelers. In the 1960s it was the Packers, and I think Green Bay was the first NFL dynasty that people will look at.

Adam Timmerman

Offensive guard

His teams: *Green Bay Packers 1995-98; St. Louis Rams 1999-2006*

FACING THE GREEN BAY PACKERS

His view: Even visiting teams could feel the home-field advantage Lambeau gave the Packers.

WE DIDN'T PLAY there a lot when I was with the Rams; I think once or twice. But the guys who had never been there, they knew I'd played there, and they'd ask me what it was like. I told them it was a special place.

I definitely remember playing in Lambeau, and it was definitely different as an opposing player. It was weird walking out of the opposite tunnel, because for the first few years of my career I'd come out of the other one, and people used to cheer for me. Now I was coming out of the other, and they weren't.

You always felt such a strong home-field advantage when I played there, but you could also feel the advantage they had as an opposing player. And I probably felt it more so because I had been on the other sideline.

But the fans were still great to me even though I was playing for the Rams. They were always good sports about it. They would holler some things, but mostly it was the "welcome back" kind of thing. It was all good things, and that just kind of reinforced the way I felt when I played there. I didn't really want to leave, but football was a business, and you do what's best for your family. But even being an Iowa kid, Green Bay was always home to me.

You'd see former players in St. Louis who had played for the Rams, but then you'd see former Packers at Lambeau Field, and they were in their sixties, seventies, and eighties. And these were guys everybody knew. The history of the league went a lot farther back with the Packers than it did with the Rams.

When you're in Green Bay, you don't get out quite so much. You don't go to the Packers Hall of Fame or the restaurants. But you know all about it, and it has such a deep history.

My wife and I say every player in the NFL should play in Green Bay for at least one year to appreciate how different it is. But it was different in a good way.

Luther Elliss

Defensive end/tackle

His teams: Detroit Lions 1995-2003; Denver Broncos 2004
His view: Packers fans not only rooted for their team at home but traveled well, too.

FIRST AND FOREMOST, it's the mystique. It's Lambeau Field, and that says it all. It's the frozen tundra, and this is where the history of the NFL takes place, I think. It's one of the building blocks of the NFL.

As a kid watching those NFL Films, you'd think, "Wow, those are true warriors." That's one of the intriguing things about football: You have those old films to remind you that if you wanted to be a warrior or a tough guy, that was the way to go. You played at Lambeau Field.

For me, it was more the mystique. I didn't need to play for the Packers to feel that it was just playing there. It was also about

117

the fans. The fans are unbelievable there. I remember you'd pull into Appleton the day before the game (where the visiting team hotel was located), and there wasn't much going on. But the next morning, there's this big ruckus going on in the lobby. It's green and gold, and it's the Packers. The whole town got transformed. It was like a little fairy waved a wand, and it was game day.

That kind of stuff got me excited and got me ready to play. I love fans like that. Blue collar fans who love and appreciate what you do.

It was the same when we played them in Detroit. I remember there weren't a lot of blue jerseys in the stands when I first started there. There were times, when we weren't doing so well, that I think Lions fans flipped their jersey at halftime, and it was one of those times when we wish we had fans like they did in Green Bay. It was kind of discouraging when we'd hear Packers fans cheering in our stadium, and it was like, "really?"

As time went by and we got better, Lions fans got better, too. But I don't think there are too many teams whose fans travel as well as the Packers fans do. Maybe the Steelers, but that's about it. And a lot of times they're not even at the game. It was like, oh my gosh, they didn't even go to the game, but they still came to the city where the Packers were playing. It's just such devotion to a team.

Tom Thayer
Offensive guard

His team: Chicago Bears 1985-92; Miami Dolphins 1993

His view: It always meant a lot to us to win in Green Bay.

WE WERE EXPECTED to go up there and win games. It meant a lot to the Bears to go up there and win. I remember the only game I lost up there was that Don Majkowski game in 1989. They were always hard fought, and we always walked out of there a confident group of guys.

Scott Mitchell

Quarterback

His teams: Miami Dolphins 1991-93; Detroit Lions 1994-98; Baltimore Ravens 1999; Cincinnati Bengals 2000-01
His view: Playing at Milwaukee County Stadium was an experience like few others.

IT'S ALWAYS HARDER to play anywhere on the road, just from the noise standpoint. You just can't come off the ball quite as quick. But then you have Lambeau Field. Absolutely, there is a mystique there, and those Packers always felt that they don't lose here. It's Lambeau Field. Come on! It's the frozen tundra, and that's going to play into every visiting team's psyche. On top of that it's this rinky-dink locker room, and you stay at a hotel in Appleton, which is like an hour away.

Still, Lambeau was far and away my favorite place to play. It's located right in a neighborhood. There are all these houses, and then all of a sudden up pops this massive stadium. It's Vince Lombardi. People think this is our hometown, it's really our team. I mean, we had people in Michigan who were Packers fans.

I remember my first game in Milwaukee. *(Author's note: The Packers played two games a season in Milwaukee, first at State Fair Park and then Milwaukee County Stadium starting in 1933, to expand the team's fan base and as a thank-you to Milwaukee residents for supporting the struggling franchise financially in the 1930s. But it became economically untenable in the 1990s to keep playing in a small stadium configured for baseball. The Packers played their last season at County Stadium in 1994, the final memorable game coming December 18 on Brett Favre's last-minute touchdown dive against the Atlanta Falcons that vaulted the Packers into the playoffs. As a nod to fans in the southern part of the state, the Packers still provide two games a season for Milwaukee season-ticket holders.)*

It's one of those games where you feel like you're waking up in a bad dream. Both teams were on the same sideline, and you're looking right at the enemy. It was really strange. I remember I broke my wrist in that game. Tackle Lomas Brown was quoted as saying he didn't block his guy so I'd get hurt, but I don't think he really did that.

But just playing in a place like that tells you a lot about the Packers. They wanted their fan base to have a special experience, and what owner in his right mind would ever do that if not to give fans the best experience possible?

I hated the Packers. I didn't like any of my opponents. I had the mindset that "I just don't like you guys." I wasn't into the buddy thing at the end of a game. I didn't stop and talk with the other guys after the game. They were the enemy and I wanted to beat them, and if we lost I was in no mood to be nice. That's the way it was with guys like Brett Favre. I might cordially say congratulations after the game, but that was about it. I thought he was a hilarious guy, but I hated Brett Favre and every other player, because I was trying to beat them.

Brent Jones

Tight end

His team: San Francisco 49ers 1987-97
His view: When Mike Holmgren came in as head coach and Brett Favre took over as quarterback, that's when the metamorphosis of the Packers began.

WE STARTED SEEING their improvement in 1994. I personally felt they had two pieces that were significant to their future. The first was Mike Holmgren and the second was Brett Favre, a young Brett Favre. Having seen those two guys in action and knowing Mike's awareness, I knew it gave them a huge advantage when we played.

Tom Thayer
Offensive guard

His team: Chicago Bears 1985-92; Miami Dolphins 1993
His view: Playing in Green Bay reminds me of a college atmosphere.

I GREW UP IN Joliet, Illinois, so as a kid, the NFC Central Division was a big part of my life. I knew all about the teams in that division. The first game I ever went to, I think I was sixteen, and I think it was a preseason game. Lynn Dickey was the quarterback for the Packers, but the whole ideal of the Packers for me started with the Vince Lombardi time. The championships, how tough he was, and you thought if you liked football, you wanted to think you were tough enough to play for that guy. And that continued when I went to Notre Dame. It was just that special.

For me, the two greatest places for fans to watch a football game are Notre Dame against USC at the Rose Bowl and the Packers playing the Bears at Lambeau Field. I played in that stadium in the '80s, and I've seen the development of Lambeau over the years. It's so much different now, but in terms of interaction with the fans, it's still great.

But I think it's more about the city of Green Bay than the stadium itself. The stadium is the center of the city, but Green Bay still has the same loyal fan base. They can't wait to get to their parking location. Notre Dame was similar to that.

People would come in from all over the country to go to Notre Dame games, and it was similar in Green Bay. It was just like a college atmosphere, and I loved it. Everybody converges, and then they leave. It's just neat to see what the stadium means to the area.

Steve Mariucci

His teams: Quarterbacks coach–Green Bay Packers 1992-95; Head coach–San Francisco 49ers 1997-2002; Head coach–Detroit Lions 2003-05
His view: Growing up a Packers fan, I found the team's history especially significant.

I'M ACTUALLY SITTING in my office in California as I'm talking to you, and I have photos of me as a kid (he grew up in the Upper Peninsula of Michigan) getting autographs of Paul Hornung, Jim Taylor, Willie Wood, and Herb Adderley. I grew up a Packers fanatic.

I actually saw two games growing up. We went to training camp for practice all the time, and I went to two preseason games as a kid, and for one it rained so hard, we had to sit in the Lambeau Field tunnel. Then we got on the field and got some pictures by the goal post. I didn't go to a regular season game until I was coaching. That was that first time I ever got to do that.

FACING THE GREEN BAY PACKERS

I could name every player from those great teams of the '60s. I could do it for you right now. I was obsessed. These were my heroes, my idols, and going down and getting autographs, that stays alive in you forever. I know these guys.

I just had my 60th birthday party with Bart Starr and his wife, Cherry, and he was so cordial. And Bart (who suffered a stroke earlier in the year) ended up making it to the Brett Favre number retirement on Thanksgiving night.

Bart was my hero as a nine-year-old, and he still is. I got to watch him when I was a coach at Northern Michigan. He was still the coach of the Packers. I remember I went down to training camp at St. Norbert College, and he greeted us and said, "Welcome to St. Norbert. Glad to have you here." He was such a gentleman. He was always a gentleman.

I remember when I began coaching with Mike (Holmgren) in Green Bay, it was like a dream come true for me. I remember the gold *G* in the carpeting, and late at night I'd walk down the hall and walk the facility, and I'd take it all in and say, "I can't believe I'm working for the Green Bay Packers." Talk about a dream come true. It absolutely was. For a kid from the Upper Peninsula, this was it. And when they remodeled the locker room, I grabbed some of that carpeting and I kept it with me for years. My wife finally got disgusted with it and threw it out. That really bummed me out.

Steve McMichael

Defensive tackle/nose tackle

His teams: New England Patriots 1980; Chicago Bears 1981-93; Green Bay Packers 1994
His view: Long-time Bear had no second thoughts finishing career in Green Bay.

THE BEARS SAID, "You've lost a step," and decided not to re-sign me, so the Packers offered me money and I still wanted to play. So I went up there. Sure, I'd played with the Bears for twelve years, but to hear that crowd again, I wanted to keep it alive. I just wasn't finished yet. So I went up to Green Bay on my last leg and stole their money, and, on one leg, we kicked the Bears' asses. I had no second thoughts about it. *(Author's note: Figuratively on one leg, McMichael played in all sixteen games, starting fourteen, and recorded 19 tackles and 2.5 quarterback sacks.)*

Some Bears fans had a real problem with it, especially playing for the Packers, but I explained that I really needed to hear that crowd again. It was that same ferocity and same angst that I'd always had, because that's what fuels the warrior. It's the fear of failure. That's the same with any pro football player. You're not scared of the other team, but you're afraid of failing in front of the world. Oh man, I had nightmares about that. But I enjoyed my year in Green Bay. Then I knew it was time to retire.

Mark Brunell

Quarterback

His teams: Green Bay Packers 1993-94; Jacksonville Jaguars 1995-2003; Washington Redskins 2004-06; New Orleans Saints 2008-09; New York Jets 2010-11

His view: The Packers were a big-time team in a very small market.

WHEN I GOT drafted by the Packers, I was thrilled. I wasn't a high draft pick, but I was fortunate and thankful Mike Holmgren took a chance on me. It was funny because my wife said before the draft, "I don't care where you go. I just hope it isn't Green Bay. It's so cold there."

I didn't know a lot about the Packers. I went to college in Seattle (University of Washington), so I wasn't exposed to a lot of that as a kid. But when I got to Green Bay, I made a point of going to the Packers Hall of Fame, and I saw just how special it was.

I probably didn't know anything more about the Packers than any other kid who grew up in Southern California. You knew the history and the tradition a bit, but if I'd grown up in Wisconsin, it would have been a different story. But like anybody who followed NFL football, I knew enough to know that Green Bay was a special place.

Green Bay was unlike any other organization. It's a very unique place. It's a big-time team in a very small market.

Harry Sydney

Fullback

His teams: San Francisco 49ers 1987-91; Green Bay Packers 1992
His view: Change of attitude and perception no longer made Green Bay the Siberia of the NFL.

YOU WERE ALWAYS looking at a team that could win, but Green Bay back in the '80s was a team, and so were the Minnesota Vikings to an extent, where players went to disappear. It was Siberia. It wasn't a destination job. When I was with the 49ers, we feared the cold more than we did the Green Bay Packers.

I want to say we played them in 1986 and 1987, and again in 1989, and we should have beaten them in '89. That's when we played them when they had Don Majkowski at quarterback, and the wind was really blowing. I remember that. We didn't take them for granted, but they were a team that just wasn't winning. It was like taking a break when we played the Packers.

I really didn't learn much about Green Bay until I started playing with them, and then coaching them and living there. I had to learn all about the "Ice Bowl." You don't have time to pay attention to other teams when you're playing, but once I got here I learned a lot about it.

My perception when I got here in '92 was, in my mind, "What's this?" You have to remember, we were the San Francisco 49ers. It was top notch, top of the line.

I didn't go to training camp with the Packers that year, because I was cut in training camp by the 49ers. So I remember one practice, (linebacker) Bryce Paup was there, and he was practicing like practice was a game. He didn't even know how to practice. None of them really did. It's about a mindset. It was the whole philosophy on how to win that they had to learn.

Mike (Holmgren) had learned that with Bill Walsh in San Francisco, and he brought that to Green Bay. And when you witness the transformation, to be part of that is kind of gratifying. That first year in Green Bay was interesting.

That season I was kind of a semi-player/coach. Gil Haskell was our offensive coordinator, but he really didn't know the West Coast offense. I knew every aspect of it. I said to Gil, "You have to ask me how to handle the offense. You're teaching the plays, but the guys are looking to *me* for answers because I've played in it for so long."

Mike's attitude was always, if a player screws up he'd yell at the coach. (Former Packers assistant coach) Andy Reid had a place where he'd always get chewed out. A lot of that was orchestrated by Mike. But he did change the attitude. I came over to Green Bay because I saw what Mike was trying to do. I was fortunate.

Ron Wolf

His teams: Personnel director Oakland-Los Angeles Raiders, 1963-74, 1979-89; Tampa Bay Buccaneers 1976-78; New York Jets 1990-91; General manager–Green Bay Packers 1991-2001
His view: I wanted a chance to prove I could run my own team, and this was the perfect opportunity.

I **WANTED THE OPPORTUNITY** to prove I had the capability to run an NFL franchise. When I left the Raiders in 1990, I went to the Jets in New York, and I thought I'd be a personnel director for the rest of my career. Then I'd ride off into the sunset. That's pretty much what I thought.

Then something happened. George Young was hired to be general manager of the New York Giants, and Dick Steinberg was hired by the Jets. And they were about the same age as me, and I thought I could do that, too. So when Bob Harlan offered me the opportunity, I was not going to turn it down.

And the thing is, I really didn't know anything about the Packers. I truly didn't. So I'm driving with Lee Remmel (the Packers' long-time PR director), and you know Lee, he's a walking history of the Green Bay Packers. So he's telling me all the things that the Packers haven't accomplished over the years, and I'm saying, "You've got to be kidding me."

But what motivated me was to prove *I could do it.* That was my motivation. I had the very good fortune of being able to get up there before Thanksgiving, and that gave me a chance to see four or five games. I had an insight on that football team.

And what I realized is that the Packers needed a quarterback, so I went out and got one.

And do you know what my biggest thrill was in all my years in football? It was standing on the sideline at Lambeau Field at the end of the NFC Championship Game against Carolina for the right to go to the Super Bowl. It was an incredible moment.

I learned this is a very special place. I didn't realize what I was getting into, because, as I said, I really didn't know anything about Green Bay or the Green Bay Packers. I remember I watched this show on TV called "Grandstand Franchise." It was about the Packers. It was narrated by Ray Scott, and it was about three hours long. That's when I became a huge Green Bay Packers fan. I felt I learned a lot about the history of the Green Bay Packers, and what they meant to the entire National Football League.

Let's not sugarcoat this. The Packers are the crown jewel of the National Football League, and Lambeau Field is a professional football cathedral. If one has the opportunity to work in that organization, you can't help but feel you're sort of special... and to be a part of the green and gold, it's incredible.

Facing the Packers Defense

SCOTT MITCHELL

Quarterback

His team: Miami Dolphins 1991-93; Detroit Lions 1994-98; Baltimore Ravens 1999; Cincinnati Bengals 2000-01
His view: Defensive coordinator Fritz Shurmur was the key to the Packers' dominance.

YOU ALWAYS HAD to account for (defensive end) Reggie White. Then there was Sean Jones on the other side, who was pretty darned good, too. I remember we had a pretty underrated tackle named Zefross Moss. We felt like he could handle Reggie all by himself, because he was pretty stout by himself. But if you did that, who would account for Sean Jones? That was a really good defense then.

They always had some great players in their secondary, and they were one of the first teams to play us completely different than anybody else because of Barry Sanders.

A lot of that was on (Packers defensive coordinator) Fritz Shurmur. He did some great things. They completely revised their structure to defended Barry, and it was pretty simple. They were going to force Barry to run from tackle to tackle. They didn't do it all the time, but I remember they did a good job of forcing Barry to do something he didn't want to do, and that was run tackle to tackle.

Barry Sanders was like Babe Ruth, because he'd swing for the fences on every play. He was trying to score touchdowns on every play. He'd go inside and the defense would pursue him, and then he'd cut back. Like Babe Ruth, he also struck out a lot. But when he broke it, it was beautiful to see. He did that a few times against the Packers, but not as often as he wanted to.

When we had our best success, it's when we didn't try to force Barry on people. We let the game come to him. We didn't try to force Barry down peoples' throats. I think the Packers understood that very well.

And that defense in the mid-'90s was very good, very underrated. They had (380-pound nose tackle) Gilbert Brown in the middle, and he was like two people. Really great teams have guys like that in the interior.

You needed someone inside, and then you needed really athletic rush ends, and the Packers had that with Reggie and Sean Jones. Then you needed really active linebackers who can move laterally, and while they didn't get a lot of notoriety, the Packers had good, active linebackers like George Koonce. That's when Green Bay, in my opinion, was at its best.

They had some other underrated guys, too. (Cornerback) Doug Evans was a player who comes to mind, and (safety) Darren Sharper was just coming into his own, too. A safety is the anchor of your defense, and Leroy Butler was special. If you want to talk about a special player, Leroy Butler was it. He was the defense.

I remember we were playing them in 1998, and I had what I thought was a wide-open touchdown pass, and he comes over and makes just a spectacular play. I thought it was a touchdown. But that's what special players do.

PAUL GRUBER

Left tackle

His team: Tampa Bay Buccaneers 1988-99
His view: The Packers defense could always make a play when it had to.

I RECALL PRIMARILY SEAN Jones. Sean was a really good player for a long time; I used to play against him when he was in Houston. He was one of the top defensive ends in the league, and when he went to the Packers, I think that was a big piece for them. And since all the protections were designed around stopping Reggie, I would go against Sean one-on-one the whole game. I felt I played pretty well against him.

They were stout up the middle, and it was tough to run against them. They had great leadership on defense starting with Reggie White, and Reggie could always make a play when it was needed. Reggie always seemed to make a play at the right time. So did Brett.

In the early-'90s, they had another really good player in tight end Tim Harris. He was a nonstop talker, but a high-motor guy who always kept coming after you. And linebacker Bryce Paup for a while was a really good player for them, too. Their teams just weren't quite as good. They definitely didn't have the team at the time.

133

Brent Jones
Tight end

His team: San Francisco 49ers 1987-97
His view: There just weren't many weaknesses in the Packers' defense.

MIKE HOLMGREN BROUGHT in guys who were very similar to the type of players he had in San Francisco. But Mike, to his credit, also brought in some nuances, because he was definitely his own guy.

They had a defense with guys that just didn't have many weaknesses. It was really tough to find cracks in the defense. It was one of those "bend, but don't break" defenses, and it was probably very underrated. They had some good players across the board, and (safety) Leroy Butler was probably the most underrated. He was a great player and could do so many different things. He was always someone you had to account for, and that wasn't always easy to do.

Max Lane
Offensive tackle/guard

His team: New England Patriots 1994-2000

His view: Green Bay's defense was always underrated.

WHEN YOU THINK of that Packers Super Bowl team of 1996, you didn't really look at individuals besides Reggie White on defense. I think more so it was the defense as a whole.

When people look at that team, the casual fans, they think of the Packers and think of Brett Favre. But there was a lot more to that team. The defense was the strength of that team. There wasn't a weakness on that team. There was not a weak point on that defense.

FACING BRETT FAVRE

ONLY NOW, WITH the benefit of time and perspective and with the filter of objectivity, is Brett Favre's Packers career truly ready to be appreciated. The passions have cooled, and now Favre's career can be viewed for just how amazing it truly was.

There has always been plenty of sound and fury when it comes to the Packers quarterback. He was many things to many people, depending on which side of the fence you resided.

Indeed, to many he was a competitor for the ages, a three-time league MVP who played the game the way it was meant to be played, and, most important, a winner. To just as many others, he was a reckless showboat who made mistakes at the worst time, and while he may have been the league's all-time leader in touchdown passes (before Peyton Manning took over), he is also the all-time leader in interceptions.

He has battled addiction to painkillers and the loss of his dad to produce memorable performances. He has also been vocal in his disdain to help younger quarterbacks on the team (including Aaron Rodgers), and his will-he-or-won't-he retirement games that lasted for five years, and that wore thin with even his most ardent backers.

He annoyed Packers fans, officials, and teammates in 2008, when, after retiring and changing his mind and demanding his job back, he was dealt to the New York Jets and, after that season, retired again. But he changed his mind yet again, and this time earned the unvarnished fury of Packers fans everywhere when he signed as a free agent with the hated Minnesota Vikings.

But even what he did in 2009 with Minnesota was simply magical when, at age 40, he had one of the best seasons of his career. He threw for 4,202 yards and 33 touchdowns, with just seven interceptions, as he led the Vikings to a 12-4 record and tantalizingly close to the Super Bowl.

Then came an interception on an ill-advised throw late in the NFC Championship Game against the New Orleans Saints that seemed to cement the belief that no matter how good Brett Favre could be, his mischievous angels always won out.

He played one more season in Minnesota, but injuries finally ended his remarkable streak of 321 consecutive games started, a number that may never be duplicated.

Now, comfortably ensconced in retirement and having been inducted into the Pro Football Hall of Fame in 2016, he has found a level of satisfaction.

He is comfortable with his spot in the NFL pantheon, and, most important, he has made peace with Packers fans.

In the summer of 2015, the Packers retired Favre's No. 4 in a ceremony at Lambeau Field, and a sellout crowd of more than 70,000 showed up to say thanks.

The career numbers don't matter much to Favre anymore, except for one that still gnaws at him on occasion: only one Super Bowl title.

But for Favre and his legion of fans, it was all about the game, and playing it at a level few can imagine. He was part of an era of Packers football that may never be seen again, and perhaps that matters the most.

Steve Mariucci

His teams: Quarterbacks coach–Green Bay Packers 1992-95; Head coach–San Francisco 49ers 1997-2002; Head coach–Detroit Lions 2003-05
His view: An unknown commodity at first, a friendship has grown, and a respect remains.

I **REALLY DIDN'T KNOW** anything about him until I came to the Packers. (General Manager) Ron Wolf asked me before we decided to trade for him to evaluate this quarterback he liked named Brett Favre.

I told Ron, "I'm sorry, I didn't know much about Brett Favre." I had come from the University of California, and Brett had been drafted by the Atlanta Falcons. That's all I really knew. I never watched him. So I went to watch him play, to give Ron my assessment, but Brett didn't play much in Atlanta. He threw three passes, and two of the passes were picks. It was hard to make any recommendations from that. But he wanted to have his quarterbacks coach at least take a look at him.

But I could see a few things, and I told Ron he's got a strong arm; he takes a lot chances; he's a tough guy, and he plays with a lot of emotion. That's all I could really tell him from what I'd seen. I think Ron was going to do that no matter what my evaluation was. I know how much he liked Brett, so I don't think my evaluation had anything to do with his decision. But Ron knew what he wanted.

When I left the Packers after the 1995 season, I went on to become the head coach at Cal (University of California) for a year. Then I went to the 49ers in 1997 as head coach, but I stayed in touch with Brett quite a bit.

When I was at Cal I was neutral, so we'd talk a lot. But now it's the next year and I'm with the Niners, and I'm with the enemy. I remember in 1997, when we played the Packers in the NFC Championship game. That's when Brett was in his prime. I mean, he was in the third year of his winning three straight league MVPs, and he was at his peak. The Packers were a scary offense; they could score points, and they had the best guy in Brett.

The defense was a little bit like the Niners defense with (former head coach) Bill Walsh. Nobody talked enough about the Niners defense, and it's the same with those Packers. It was an excellent defense, and Fritz Shurmur was as good a defensive coordinator as you're ever going to find. Boy, those Packers really had our number in the regular season.

I have a picture in my office where I was standing at the pregame warm-ups before a regular season game between us and the Packers in 1998. I'm playing catch with (quarterback) Steve Young, and suddenly some balls go flying by me. I look over, and Favre's on the other side of the field and he's throwing balls at me. He comes over and says, "Get Steve and let's get a picture." So (Packers team photographer) Vernon Biever took a picture of the three of us at the 50-yard line. It was just like old friends. It was crazy. It's a classic photo of the three of us. But that was Brett. Before a game, and he wants to get a photo. And the Packers beat us.

Tom Thayer

Offensive guard

His team: Chicago Bears 1985-92; Miami Dolphins 1993
His view: His performance against the Bears on a badly sprained ankle was one for the ages.

OF COURSE I never played against him as a defensive player, but I always watched him. I was kind of jealous in a sense, because he enjoyed the game so much and he was so good. Every team in the league is so desperate for a quarterback, and the Packers happened to hit on Brett Favre. And then, of course, they got Aaron Rodgers. The quarterback position is so impressive in Green Bay.

But I remember one game in particular (1995) when he played us. He had sprained his ankle really badly the week before, and I heard that he could barely walk. So we played up there the next week, and I was watching him in pregame warmups and he's limping really badly, and I'm thinking there's no way he can play.

So they go in the locker room right before the start of the game, and he comes out and he starts running around. I couldn't believe it, and I said, "Uh-oh, this is not good." *(Favre did play and threw five touchdown passes in a 35-28 win over the Bears.)*

Gary Plummer

Linebacker

His teams: San Diego Chargers 1986-93; San Francisco 49ers 1994-97
His view: He was a quarterback who could make a play out of nothing.

I HAVE A LOT of Brett Favre stories. I remember one was in the NFC Championship Game, I think it was 1996, and the Packers had a pretty good lead. It was fourth-and-inches, and I pretty much knew he was going to go with a hard count and try and get us to jump offside (for the first down). He was so good with those hard counts.

So he goes into his cadence, and I yell out, "Watch for the hard count." On the line, I see our defensive tackle Dana Stubblefield getting jumpy and ready to go, so I grab him by the belt of his pants to keep him from going offside. And I see Brett smirking. So he goes back through his cadence again, and then our other defensive tackle, Bryant Young, starts getting jumpy, too. So I grab him by the belt, too. So I've got hold of these two guys by the belt. Brett cracks up and calls time out.

That just showed me the way he played the game. He loved the game. He had this child-like enthusiasm.

And there was another game, the NFC Championship Game in 1997 at Candlestick. It was a play-action pass, and they ran a lead draw at me. My job was to be the smashmouth guy. They had obviously watched how hard I came up to the line of scrimmage.

It must have been somewhere around our 5-yard line, and I met their fullback in the hole.

I knew they were trying to throw to their tight end in the end zone, and I recognized it at the last second. So I dropped back and got my hand up and nicked the ball, and it was incomplete. Brett looks at me, and he puts his thumb and index up about a quarter inch apart and stares at me and smiles.

He was the kind of guy you hated playing against, because he always made something out of nothing. But you also enjoyed playing against him, because he wasn't a jerk about it. He loved the game so much. The biggest thing was his ability to extend plays.

I remember another play, in that same NFC Championship Game at Candlestick. He was rolling to his left, and he literally slid on his knees and threw the ball 30 yards downfield and completed the pass. It was ridiculous. No one would have even attempted that pass, let alone completed it. I remember that happened, and I said to myself, "How the hell do you stop that?"

Steve McMichael
Defensive tackle/nose tackle

His teams: New England Patriots 1980; Chicago Bears 1981-93; Green Bay Packers 1994
His view: Favre played the game in such a way that his teammates did not want to let him down.

IT'S NOT JUST what he did on the field, it's how his teammates wanted to play their asses off for him. They didn't want to fail him. He's what they looked up to when they were all little kids and wanted to play pro football. He's the role model you envision as a kid.

When I was with the Bears, I could see what Brett was going to be even when he was just a kid. I knew we'd have to beat him with a baseball bat because he would never, ever give up. I remember my last game against Brett when I was with the Bears (in 1993). Our defense scored three touchdowns (Favre threw for 402 yards but also threw three interceptions, two of which were returned for touchdowns in a 30-17 Bears win). But we knew how good he was going to be. I just wish the Packers had gotten stupid and let him get traded to the Bears.

(HHHHH)

Scott Mitchell

Quarterback

His teams: Miami Dolphins 1991-93; Detroit Lions 1994-98; Baltimore Ravens 1999; Cincinnati Bengals 2000-01
His view: Favre's performance against the Oakland Raiders after his dad's death was inspirational.

THE PACKERS WERE so tough to play at Lambeau Field, but we always knew when they came to Detroit we were going to beat them. Or at least have a better chance of beat-ing them. We figured Brett would throw three interceptions and we'd beat them.

I remember watching Brett on film, and I remember think-ing there's no way this guy is going to last in the NFL, making the decisions he'd make and throwing the ball like he does. Then something clicked with him, and that's when the Packers began clicking on all cylinders.

I became the biggest Brett Favre fan in the world when his dad died, and watching him play that Monday night game in Oakland. *(Author's note: Two days after Favre's dad Ervin died of a heart attack in December 2004, Favre threw for 399 yards and five touchdowns as the Packers routed the Raiders.)*

How he played that game, and how he responded, it really hit me in a very special place and gave me a tremendous amount of respect for Brett.

Don Beebe

Wide receiver

His teams: Buffalo Bills 1989-94; Carolina Panthers 1995; Green Bay Packers 1996-97
His view: Finger surgery was a sign he was part of the Brett Favre club.

HAD HEARD WHEN I came there, if you didn't have one of your fingers broken or dislocated by one of Brett's passes, you really weren't part of the club. So you get a broken or dislocated finger from one of his throws, they're called "Favreisms."

And I was part of it because I had major surgery on the ring finger of my right hand, and it's permanently disfigured. They had to replace tendons and put four pins in the finger until it's stabilized. That's how hard Brett threw the ball. It was incredible.

He was a special guy to play with. I'll never forget Super Bowl XXXI when we beat New England. Everyone knew that I'd been to four Super Bowls and lost four when I was with the Buffalo Bills. Everybody knew the history. But on the last play, when Brett was just taking a knee to run out the clock, I was lined up in the backfield. He took the snap and came back to me and gave me the game ball and said, "Nobody's more deserving, Beebs." I didn't expect him to say that. That meant a lot to me.

Bob Lurtsema
Defensive tackle/end

His teams: New York Giants 1967-71; Minnesota Vikings 1971-76; Seattle Seahawks 1976-77

FACING THE GREEN BAY PACKERS

His view: He never cared about statistics; for him it was all about the competition.

I NEVER PLAYED AGAINST him, but I watched him when I did broadcasts for the Vikings and just as a football fan. I think I saw every game he played against the Vikings, and a lot of others, too.

And those people who criticized Brett Favre for the way he played know nothing about football. Brett Favre was everything to football. His commitment to his teammates and winning was incredible. Yes, he led the league in interceptions (he owns the NFL record for career interceptions with 336), but that's the way he played. He'd be down by ten points with a minute and a half to go, and he'll throw into a crowd to try and make something happen. He was always trying to win, and he doesn't care about stats. That's contagious with a team. When they see how dedicated you are to trying to win, the team sees that.

Critics always try to twist things around with Brett. What's that bad about interceptions anyway? He was just such a great competitor. I remember when he played for the Vikings, and the New Orleans Saints had that bounty out on him in the NFC Championship Game. They just beat the hell out of him, but he never complained. He said, "Everybody goes after the quarterback and this was no different." That's how he always approached the game. He was just a great competitor.

Adam Timmerman
Offensive guard

His teams: Green Bay Packers 1995-98; St. Louis Rams 1999-2006
His view: His leadership abilities were second to none.

WE WILL SEE another quarterback like him, but it's going to be a long time. Maybe Peyton Manning is in that mold. They are both class acts the way they handle themselves.

Brett always treated me very well. I never really got the feeling he was big-timing me. He didn't think he was bigger than anyone else. When I came in as a rookie in 1996, he was great. He was just a very unselfish guy. That's the way all of our leaders on those teams were like. That's what we had going for us. All of our leaders, including Brett, were very unselfish people.

Luther Elliss
Defensive tackle/end

His teams: Detroit Lions 1995-2003; Denver Broncos 2004
His view: He believed he could make a play at any time and often did.

YOU JUST APPRECIATE who he is. What was that they always said about him? He's a gunslinger? That's what he was. And as much as that helped us as a team, sometimes it also hurt us, because he truly believed he could make a play at any time. He proved why he's a Hall of Famer.

He played the game the way it was meant to be played, in my opinion. He played it like a child. I remember I was in my second year with the Lions, and he was going through his cadence and he'd go, "Red 80, red 80, hey, how's it going, Luther?" and I'm thinking, "What is this?" It's so out of character to do something like that, but that's because he was such a great competitor. He thoroughly enjoyed the game and he competed at such a high level, but he never got so wrapped up in it that he couldn't enjoy himself.

He was a talker, and he probably said more to me than I ever said to him. I wasn't a talker. I just tried to let my play do the talking. But when he'd talk to me, you could see that sparkle in his eye. I remember one game in Detroit, and we were up, and he had the Packers driving. I came through and really hit him. He had seen me coming, but he sat there and took the hit. That just increased my respect for him. He was a spectacle. He was something to watch, and he was fun to watch.

I think one thing that's always forgotten about him is that he was a lot quicker than people realize. He did more than enough and was quick enough to extend plays. There's a reason they called him a gunslinger. It's because it all goes back to his confidence, almost to an arrogant level. He always had confidence in himself. Our coaches always said, "He's going to make this play, so you've got to stay after him."

Mark Brunell

Quarterback

His teams: Green Bay Packers 1993-94; Jacksonville Jaguars 1995-2003; Washington Redskins 2004-06; New Orleans Saints 2008-09; New York Jets 2010-11
His view: I learned how to play the game from Brett Favre.

I LEARNED SO MUCH from Brett. I learned how to play the game. Sure, there were a lot of interceptions, but there were also a lot of touchdowns. He was also learning the game. He gave it absolutely everything he had on game day. He was calm, competitive, with an incredibly strong arm. I watched and learned from him.

Professionally, Green Bay was perfect for me to start my career, because I wasn't ready to play. So I learned a lot from Brett. He was very raw, and he was still very young then. He wasn't the quarterback then that he would become, but I could sense something special was happening with him. I learned from him that it was important to compete, and he was learning what it took to be a professional, to be a franchise quarterback.

The Packers certainly understood that Brett was going to be the guy, and there were no alternatives. He was the franchise quarterback, and from Brett's perspective he didn't want to let people down.

149

I think we played them in 1995 (when Brunell was starting for the Jacksonville Jaguars), and you could absolutely see the change in him.

In '95, you could see how his career changed. He had turned into one of the league's best quarterbacks. It wasn't just what he did but who he was. He was a different style of quarterback. He was tough and gritty, and if you needed a play, he'd make it. He wasn't your typical quarterback. The word *toughness* keeps coming up with him, and you couldn't keep him down. He'd do anything he could to win a football game.

I played nineteen years and I've had hundreds and hundreds of teammates, but Brett Favre was without a doubt the funniest guy I've ever been around. He was absolutely hilarious.

In the quarterback room, he could tell so many stories that would make you laugh. It was a great quarterback room, and I had a great relationship with all the guys. It was an ideal situation.

Mike Alstott

Fullback

His team: Tampa Bay Buccaneers 1996-2006
His view: Respect, competition fired the jawing sessions between Favre and Warren Sapp.

WE HAD SOME great games against the Packers, and what a lot of people remember is the rivalry Brett had with (the Bucs defensive tackle) Warren Sapp. Those guys were always talking to each other.

But what everyone saw between those two was really just normal conversation. They loved playing against each other, and they really respected each other. But when they'd talk back and forth, it was never anything malicious. They were just very competitive. I'm sure some words were said, but really there was just a lot of respect.

Harry Sydney

Fullback

His teams: San Francisco 49ers 1987-91; Green Bay Packers 1992

His view: He showed after a while that he was a special player.

MY FIRST IMPRESSION of Brett Favre? To be honest, just another redneck quarterback with a strong arm.

But I remember his first game against the Cincinnati Bengals. I was on the field for that last drive, and it was something. I do remember then seeing a guy with a lot of potential. You see

151

those guys all the time, but you don't really know it until they show they're going to do it.

The West Coast offense was so complicated, but I understood the offense and the checkdowns (from his years with the 49ers), and I saw this guy scrambling around and that he had that kind of potential. Imagine trying to run the West Coast offense the way Joe Montana or Steve Young did, doing it without the expectations. That was Brett that day. That's a lot of pressure.

When I became Green Bay's running backs coach (1995-99), I wasn't paying too much attention to what Brett was doing, because I was thinking about coaching my players. I didn't see how good he could be when I started coaching. Then I started paying attention, and I saw him throw the ball and the routes and the timing, and you started seeing him be serious about the game.

Ron Wolf

His teams: *Oakland-Los Angeles Raiders, personnel director 1963-74, 1979-89; Tampa Bay Buccaneers 1976-78; New York Jets 1990-91; General manager Green Bay Packers 1991-2001*
His view: *His very presence changed a game.*

PEOPLE ASK ME all the time what it was I saw in Brett Favre that maybe no one else saw. I thought the field tilted in his team's favor when he ran on it. Just by his appearance on the field, he changed everything.

Look at it this way. Before I arrived, this team had the poorest record in the National Football League, and when I left in 2001, they went from the team with the poorest record to the team with the best record. And that was because of Brett Favre. In college, he played the entire East-West (all-star) game. He beat Georgia. He beat Alabama. He changed games wherever he went. He was that special.

FACING REGGIE WHITE

IT **ALL CHANGED** for the Green Bay Packers organization with Reggie White. Hyperbole? Hardly. When in 1993 the Packers signed the most sought-after free agent in the NFL at the time, it was greeted in sports circles with a mixture of disbelief, bemusement, and cynicism. Among long-suffering Packers, the reaction was not much different.

Green Bay? Really?

White, a star defensive end for the Philadelphia Eagles, had grown frustrated with the Eagles' inability to advance in the postseason, and, after the 1992 season when his contract had run out, he was equally frustrated by the lack of progress in contract negotiations.

So he declared himself a free agent, with a part of him fully expecting the Eagles to come to their senses and re-sign him. In the meantime, he embarked on a tour around the NFL, shopping his services to teams that needed a pass-rushing juggernaut and were willing to pay what he believed he was worth.

The smart money believed it would eventually come down to the NFL's richest and most successful franchises coming through with an offer that would allow the rich to get richer. Indeed, the San Francisco 49ers and Washington Redskins appeared to be the finalists in the Reggie White derby, with the Redskins offering a four-year, $13 million deal, and the 49ers five years and $19.5 million, though not all of that contract would be guaranteed.

After all, White was already thirty-one years old, and, logic suggested, he was on the downside of his career.

Lost to the rest of the league, though, was the behind-the-scenes, quiet negotiations between White's agent and Packers officials. And when Green Bay offered a guaranteed four-year deal worth $17 million, both the 49ers and Redskins backed off.

It was the biggest contract ever offered to an NFL free agent to that point, and it immediately put the Packers on the radar.

White told the story at his introductory press conference (and hundreds of times in the years to follow) that Green Bay had been the place Eagles coaches had threatened players they'd trade them to if they didn't improve.

"But no more," he said with a smile.

He also said he'd been impressed with the Packers the season before, when the Eagles had played the Packers in Milwaukee. He remembered sacking their young quarterback, Brett Favre, and injuring the kid's shoulder. But Favre proved to be tough and resilient, and he fought back and the Packers had beaten the Eagles. That caught White's attention.

That team, and that quarterback, had stayed in White's memory, and he remembered thinking, "He's going to be special someday."

So that was another reason he cited for signing. And, as an ordained minister, White also said God had sent him signs, as well, that he should sign with the Packers.

Cynics of White's decision said there was indeed a divine sign: 17 million of them, in fact.

But whatever the reason, White changed everything for a Packers team that was starting over.

For White, it would all culminate three years later in New Orleans when, thanks to his two late sacks of New England Patriots quarterback Drew Bledsoe, the Packers won Super Bowl XXXI. And the image of White sprinting the length of the field holding aloft the Lombardi Trophy remains burned in the minds of Packers fans everywhere.

He went on to record 68.5 sacks in his six years with the Packers, which was the team record until 2008, when it was eclipsed by Kabeer Gbaja-Biamila. But more than the numbers, White's signing in Green Bay changed a culture, an attitude, a perception of Green Bay, and of the concept of free agency.

"I don't think you'll ever see free agency again like it was when Reggie signed with Green Bay," notes Max Lane, the former New England Patriots right tackle who is still dubiously, and probably unfairly, remembered as the player White steamrolled on consecutive plays to sack Bledsoe and sew up the Super Bowl win. "In 1993, it was like the true era when free agency first took hold, and it's never going to be like that again. You could say Green Bay was the last team to really take advantage of it like that."

Even today, White's signing by Green Bay is considered one the most significant in NFL history and was a graphic demonstration of what one player, properly motivated and used in the right way, can do to change the direction of a franchise.

Max Lane

Offensive guard/tackle

His team: New England Patriots 1994-2000
His view: He was simply the best to ever play the position.

OH YEAH, I still get asked about that Super Bowl all the time. I remember going into that game our tight end, Ben Coates, if he was on my side of the line of scrimmage, he was supposed to chip Reggie on his way out to his pass routes.

So the first half we had relatively little problem with Reggie. If Ben was lined up next to me, he'd chip him, and it worked out pretty well. We kind of kept Reggie off balance in the first half. I was one-on-one with Reggie half the time in the first half, and I think I did OK.

But at halftime, our tight ends coach comes over to me and says, "It looks like you're doing OK. We'd like to get Ben out in pass patterns more, so we're going to take the chip off. Are you OK with that?" So I said, "Yeah."

In the second half, we were in a position where we had to throw the ball more. And when Desmond Howard returned that kickoff for a touchdown, we were down, and we had to throw on just about every down. That was exactly what Reggie wanted.

He was at the end of his career, but he was a still a really good player. So right after that Desmond kickoff return, Reggie got me in a classic hook move the first time, and he got to Drew. The second time, I was so guarded against getting beat to the inside, he went outside. And he got to Drew again.

A lot of people ask me the best defensive lineman I played against, and it was obviously him. I remember the first play of that Super Bowl, I noticed he didn't wear anything on his arms. No gloves, no arm pads, nothing. I think he thought they'd show some sort of weakness, so he didn't wear anything.

I remember getting down in my stance, and it all happened in a flash. I remember like it was in slow motion. All of a sudden, you look up and you see his arms, and then his biceps, and he just keeps getting bigger. Because he didn't wear anything on his arms, it made him look more imposing. I'll always remember that. That guy was country strong.

I remember the next season, Bill Parcells was gone as head coach, and Pete Carroll came in. He brought in an offensive line coach who had coached for the Detroit Lions. And they brought in a right tackle from the Lions, a guy named Zefross Moss, who over the years had had pretty good success against Reggie while he was in Detroit.

So they moved me from right tackle to left guard that season, and that didn't make a lot of sense to me. I think it was a reaction to my performance in the Super Bowl. In retrospect, my best games were against AFC teams and those were the teams we played the most, so why would you make a change like that? We played the Packers that season and I was at left guard, and I really didn't face Reggie that much. But I remember they beat us pretty good up in Foxboro.

But that switch bothered me. I was pretty sensitive toward things like that. And that Super Bowl bothered me, too. Anybody who doesn't do well in something wants the opportunity at redemption. But I didn't get to have that chance.

Brent Jones

Tight end

His team: San Francisco 49ers 1987-97
His view: Reggie White made it cool to be in Green Bay.

OF COURSE, THERE'S a third distinct advantage they had, too, and that was when they got the services of Reggie White. That was the tipping point. Reggie made it cool to go to Green Bay as a free agent. The fact that Reggie would choose Green Bay, which had not been a destination any player had really wanted to go before that, changed the component.

Mike Alstott

Fullback

His team: Tampa Bay Buccaneers 1996-2006

His view: *Facing Reggie White and an experienced Packers team helped the Bucs grow up fast.*

TONY DUNGY (TAMPA BAY'S head coach) always took a different approach when it came to facing other teams. It was always about how we did our jobs, and it wasn't about the other team. He kept the focus on our assignments and our responsibilities, and how we approached them.

As a player you *understand* your opponent and you *study* your opponent, and, for me, blocking Reggie was a big challenge. For a young team going up against a more experienced one like the Packers, I think we did all right. But Reggie was always a special challenge.

But there's no question that playing against some of those great Packers teams helped us grow as a team. We grew up awful fast because we had to. It was a great division we played in, and we had to grow up if we wanted to be competitive.

Mark Brunell
Quarterback

His teams: *Green Bay Packers 1993-94; Jacksonville Jaguars 1995-2003; Washington Redskins 2004-06; New Orleans Saints 2008-09; New York Jets 2010-11*

His view: *A sack playing against him was inevitable.*

I REMEMBERED WE PLAYED the Packers the year after I left, in 1995, and I was playing for Jacksonville. I remember Reggie White sacking me, and I remember going into that game knowing Reggie White was going to sack me. I told the offensive line before the game, "Guys, give me a break, huh? Keep Reggie off me." It didn't quite work out.

But everybody knows that's why the Packers became a force. The biggest reason was that they signed Reggie White.

Luther Elliss

Defensive tackle/end

His teams: Detroit Lions 1995-2003; Denver Broncos 2004
His view: Even as an opponent, Reggie White was a role model.

O BVIOUSLY, I NEVER played against him, but I always watched him when the Packers were on defense. I was always up watching him because you gained so much watching him play. I wanted to see what the best does and how he does it. When you have greatness on the field, you should watch it.

I remember that club move of his. I tried to emulate it, but I never really could. He was just so powerful, and he was a bigger guy, so you took advantage of leverage. I would have loved to have spent a summer working out with him. I can't imagine how much I would have learned.

Reggie was a role model for me. I competed with him, but I also always took a few minutes before and after games to speak with him. They were opportunities I'll never forget. We did talk some football things, but we talked a lot of spiritual things, too.

I'll never forget we had a couple of guys on the Lions who tried to get after Reggie, taking a few cheap shots. But he always kept his composure, and he'd always win out. He'd always play at a high level.

We had so many great conversations about football, but the majority of them were spiritual. He was really a man of God. He walked the walk.

Steve Mariucci

His teams: Quarterbacks coach–Green Bay Packers 1992-95; Head coach–San Francisco 49ers 1997-2002; Head coach–Detroit Lions 2003-05
His view: A great prankster, a great friend, and a great player; his loss is still felt.

WHEN I WAS coaching in Green Bay, Reggie and I had a great relationship. He played with my kids, and my kids played with his. We had a real cool relationship.

Back then several of us coaches, many of us had several kids, and we decided to do something about it so we wouldn't have any more, if you know what I mean.

Reggie and Brett were the two pranksters on the team, and they fed off each other. They were Frick and Frack. They were Dumb and Dumber. So a lot of people back then called me by the nickname "Mooch." But Brett and Reggie, knowing what I'd done, decided to call me "Snip Doggy Dog," and they'd make a scissors motion near their legs. That was just the way those guys were.

So fast-forward a year later and I'm coaching the San Francisco 49ers, and we're playing in the NFC Championship in the rain at Candlestick Park. It was just miserable. They were handling us pretty good in that game, and when Reggie would make a tackle or a quarterback sack, he would stop on several occasions and look over to me on the sideline. He'd find me on the sideline, and he'd go, "Hey, Snip?" and use that scissors motion down by his leg. My players saw it, and they said to me, "Hey Coach, I think Reggie is talking to you." I'd say, "Just ignore it." But that's the kind of guy Reggie was. He was just a lot of fun and, of course, a great player.

As everyone knows, Reggie's religion was very important to him (he was an ordained minister). It's who he was. When we'd play at Milwaukee County Stadium, we would have bus rides down to Milwaukee three times a year. I was sitting next to Reggie on one trip, and I remember he was really adamant about women (reporters) not being allowed in the locker room. He had a mother and wife and daughter, and it was something that was really important to him.

I asked him where his religious beliefs came from, and he showed me his Bible. And in his Bible every single page was written on, it was highlighted, it had notes in the margins. It looked like he'd read through it fifty times. It was so well read.

And when he spoke about a chapter in the Bible, he was speaking from having read it and understood it. So anyone who didn't think he was sincere about his religion didn't know him.

I remember after he retired, Reggie came out to visit us in Detroit when I coached the Lions. My players were in awe of him. I said, "Can you come out and help me coach these guys for a few days?" and he said he'd love to help out.

It was a just a few days later when he died. *(Author's note: White died December 26, 2004, from a heart attack. He was just forty-three year old. In honor of White's career, the Pro Football Hall of Fame waived the usual five-year waiting period after retirement for a player to be eligible for election. White was a first-ballot selection in February 2006 and was inducted into the Pro Football Hall of Fame that August.)*

His death was just devastating. I remember we had a game (against the Chicago Bears) the day he died, and I told our offensive coordinator Sherm Lewis that he had to call the plays that day. I told him, "I can't call the plays today. I just can't focus." It was just awful, and a loss for so many people.

FACING THE LAMBEAU FIELD WEATHER

IT WAS NEVER news that to play a game in Green Bay, Wisconsin, in November, December, or January (and occasionally in October) was never going to be a bargain. It was nature and geography, and that's the way it was, and opposing players would often look at the new season's schedule to see if they had to play in Green Bay late in the season.

FACING THE GREEN BAY PACKERS

The realization that such a game awaited was often greeted with a resigned shake of the head and the understanding that, very likely, they'd have to prepare for conditions they rarely saw elsewhere.

They had heard the stories growing up. They had seen NFL Films' tales of the "frozen tundra" of Lambeau Field, and how it could wear down even the toughest player.

The expected cold weather was bad enough. But opposing players also knew they'd have to play in a venue that was one of the toughest in the NFL, with fans who began roaring for their team two hours before the game started and who didn't stop until two hours after it was over. On top of that, the Packers had developed into one of the league's most consistent teams, and to win at Lambeau would require a special effort.

And, sometimes, that effort was hard to muster in below-zero temperatures.

There were more than a few games that Packers players could sense, even before the contest had started, that the team on the other sideline wanted no part of the conditions awaiting them on the field.

Opponents all came to Lambeau for late-season games saying what they needed to say: that the weather was no factor, and that both teams had to play in the same elements. But the Packer players knew better. They knew it was merely brave talk, and they knew that they possessed a home-field advantage like no other.

"The weather always worked to our advantage," recalls former safety Leroy Butler. "And we used it every chance we could."

Gary Plummer

Linebacker

His teams: San Diego Chargers 1986-93; San Francisco 49ers
1994-97
His view: The NFC playoff game weather in 1996 was not fit for
man nor beast.

WE PLAYED IN the playoffs (in 1996) at Lambeau, and
that was just the worst. I'd played in 24 below wind chill
before, but it was not nearly as bad as Lambeau that day.

*(Author's note: In what some long-time Packers observers still con-
sider one of the worst weather game days in team history, the Packers
faced the San Francisco 49ers in the NFC divisional semi-finals
on January 4, 1997. Snow wasn't the issue on this day, but a driving, freezing rainstorm was. In addition, the temperature was 34
degrees, but a stiff wind drove the wind chill to below zero. Meteo-
rologists at the time said that if the temperature had dropped another
three degrees, the rain would have turned to snow and could have
dropped fifteen inches on the area. Players actually said afterward
they would have preferred that to the soaking rain, which forced
both teams to scrap their complex, high-flying offenses in favor of
simply hanging onto the ball. The 49ers committed five turnovers
and the Packers just one, and Green Bay won the game, 35-14.)*

The rain soaked right through to your bones. I remember
I stood on the sideline with (linebacker) Ken Norton and

Dwain Board, our defensive line coach. We were standing in front of these 100,000-BTU heaters, and I smelled something that was burning. I look over and Dwain Board's coat is on fire, and he doesn't even know it. I couldn't believe it, but it was kind of funny.

It was the worst weather game I've ever played in my life, bar none. It was the only game I ever thought about not going back out on the field after halftime.

I remember when we got in the locker room at halftime, I went into a hot shower with my uniform on. It just didn't matter, because I was soaked anyway. I just needed to try and warm up. I changed my socks and t-shirt, but I showered with the uniform on. It was absolutely brutal.

Paul Gruber

Offensive tackle

His team: Tampa Bay Buccaneers 1988-99
His view: As a Wisconsin kid, playing in the cold was actually preferable.

I THOUGHT IT WAS awesome to play in that environment. I actually preferred the cold weather. I looked forward to it, because it always seemed we played there late in the season. I don't know why. I know we played a couple of playoff games there, and I loved it. I preferred the cold weather to sweating my butt off in Tampa.

Vince Workman
Running back

His teams: Green Bay Packers 1989-92; Tampa Bay Buccaneers 1993-94; Carolina Panthers 1995; Indianapolis Colts 1995-96
His view: Cold weather provides mental, not physical, advantage for the Packers.

IT WAS FUNNY. When I was with the Bucs, there were a couple of rookies on the team from the University of Miami. It was late in the season. I think it was November, and the temperature was probably in the 20s. These guys were really concerned about the weather, because they had never experienced playing in it. I told them to just focus on the game. That's all you could do.

I was sleeveless because I'd experienced it all before. This was no big deal. But these guys thought they were in hell. They stood by the heater shivering. I remember they both dropped a couple of passes, because, for them, it was more mental than physical. That's the advantage the Packers have always had in cold weather.

Brent Jones
Tight end

His team: San Francisco 49ers 1987-97
His view: An awful weather day led to a worse performance.

OH YEAH, I remember that playoff game in Green Bay. That one I remember vividly. We felt like the Packers might be our best matchup, but the week before, our quarterback, Steve Young, broke his ribs and tried to play with a shot of Novocain. He really couldn't do it. Elvis Grbac had to come, and we just never recovered.

That was just a rough day, because that was some of the worst weather I can ever remember. Freezing rain is the worst you can play in. I never could warm up. It was just an awful day, and we played badly.

Mike Alstott
Fullback

His team: Tampa Bay Buccaneers, 1996-2006

His view: A Chicago kid had no trouble with the sometimes fear-some elements. His teammates? That's another story.

I REMEMBER ONE YEAR we went up there to play, and it looked all nice and sunny on TV. But it was actually 15 below. I admit that was pretty cold, but I was from Chicago, so I was used to it. But a lot of guys on the team weren't. These were Florida guys, and they'd never experienced anything like it. For them it was really cold. But you can't explain it until you go through it.

Extra Point:

The Guy who Made Brett Favre's Career

All these years later, Tim Krumrie is still waiting for Brett Favre to say, "Thank you."

"I'm responsible for Brett Favre's career," recalls Krumrie, a Wisconsin native, in a tone that seems only half-kidding.

"What people really don't know is, I was responsible for putting that guy in the Hall of Fame," he adds.

Krumrie roars with laughter.

Of course, no one, and certainly not even the former All-Pro Cincinnati Bengals defensive lineman, could ever have envisioned that a particular September afternoon in 1992 at Lambeau Field would lead to a sea change, not only in the Packers organization, but in the NFL.

The 1992 season was a new start in many ways for the Packers. New general manager Ron Wolf, given unprecedented powers by team president Bob Harlan, had wasted little time firing Lindy Infante as head coach (just two years earlier, fans had voted Infante the greatest coach in Packers history in a *Milwaukee Journal* poll) and hired the hottest coaching prospect in the NFL, Mike Holmgren.

Barely a week later, with Holmgren's OK, Wolf traded a first-round draft pick to the Atlanta Falcons for a talented but unknown quarterback named Brett Favre, who was languishing on the Falcons bench.

In April, Wolf began to remake the Packers roster, drafting cornerback Terrell Buckley with their first-round selection; drafting other components for the future like tight end Mark Chmura, running back Edgar Bennett, and wide receiver Robert Brooks; and bringing in wily veterans like fullback Harry Sydney, who knew how to win and could translate that to a young roster.

But by the start of the season in September, it seemed all that hard work and optimism would be for nothing. An overtime home loss to the Minnesota Vikings started the season, and an embarrassing 31-3 road loss to the Tampa Bay Buccaneers made it appear as if this season would be more of the same.

That Tampa Bay game was especially horrifying, as Favre, making his first appearance for the Packers in a late mop-up role, actually completed his first NFL pass to himself: his pass was tipped and landed back in his arms.

"I was already beginning to wonder if I'd ever win a game in this league before I got fired," Holmgren recalled later.

The Packers returned home for their next game on September 20 against the Cincinnati Bengals, a veteran team two years removed from a playoff berth, but seeking a new direction of their own.

For Holmgren and his fragile new team, a win was crucial to restore confidence. And at that stage, Holmgren was still convinced veteran quarterback Don Majkowski was the right guy to lead the offense. He just wasn't quite as convinced as he had been when the season began.

Majkowski was not his guy. He had not coached him before. He was not the kind of quarterback who had run Holmgren's version of the so-called "West Coast offense" before. More important, he was not the quarterback his boss had given to him, at the cost of a first-round draft pick.

Since joining the Packers in 1987, Majkowski had developed a following in Green Bay. In 1989, he threw for more than 4,000 yards and 27 touchdowns, and engineered a half-dozen stirring late-game wins to earn the nickname "Majik Man." And even if he hadn't done all of that, he had secured his place in Packers fans' hearts as the quarterback who threw that epic touchdown pass to beat the Chicago Bears in the infamous "replay" game.

But that was all long ago and far away.

A bitter training camp holdout the following season blunted any momentum the Packers might have had heading into 1990. And when Majkowski did finally return, he was not the same player. Injuries then bedeviled him the rest of that season, and for much of the 1991 campaign, as well.

With the regression of Majkowski under center, the results on the field weren't pretty. After going 10-6 in 1989, the Packers plummeted back to 6-10 and then 4-12, and, with that, change came swiftly and dramatically.

While Wolf and Holmgren remade much of the roster in 1992, Majkowski remained the most veteran and viable option at quarterback until Favre was ready. The trouble was that no one really knew when (or if) that would happen.

In the meantime, the 1992 season was already in danger of spiraling out of control.

With few options, Holmgren again went with Majkowski to face the 2-0 Bengals, even though he had been less than scintillating in his first two starts, completing 37 of 53 passes for just 264 yards, with two touchdowns and two interceptions in that time.

The feeling among many who watched the Packers was that Holmgren was dying to start Favre but just couldn't bring himself to do it. The young quarterback was still unpredictable, too green, too everything.

There would come a time of Holmgren's choosing when Favre would step in and show what he could do. But this was not yet that time.

That's when fate or karma or bad luck, or a simple right turn in circumstances, changed everything. And that's where Tim Krumrie, wittingly or not, changed the course of a game, of a franchise, and of a league.

It wasn't much of a play, really.

"I was just trying to get the quarterback, and I was on the ground, and I just kind of rolled into him," Krumrie recalls. "I don't think I even had my arms around him. I just kind of knocked into him. That's just football."

It came barely five minutes into the game when Krumrie, at 6-foot-2 and 280 pounds, rolled into Majkowski's left ankle, sending the quarterback to the ground in agony. The injury proved to be torn ligaments, which promised not only to end his day, but, likely, his season.

And as Majkowski was helped off the field, Favre sprinted on, ready for the first meaningful action of his NFL career.

For the Packers and for the NFL, nothing would be the same, though Krumrie and his unsuspecting teammates wouldn't know that at the time.

"A lot of times teams don't focus on a backup quarterback," Krumrie said. "Actually, I don't even like to say backups, because everybody's a starter; everybody might play. That's the way it is in the NFL. Now we're saying, 'What the heck?' Well, we didn't say that exactly, but we said 'Who is this?' Here's this wild kid throwing the ball all over the place, and I'm saying, 'We're in trouble if we don't get it together.'"

It is now part of Packers lore that Favre, with just a slight grasp of the intricacies of Holmgren's beloved and complicated offense, was indeed throwing the ball all over the place.

As Holmgren is fond of recalling, his excitable young quarterback was calling plays for formations that did not even exist. Favre would change plays and change them back, and he would whistle passes past unsuspecting receivers who didn't even expect the ball to come to them.

Steve Mariucci was the Packers quarterbacks coach in those days, responsible for finding a way to rein in a quarterback who was apt to do anything at just about any time.

"That game against Cincinnati is when I knew we had something special," Mariucci recalled. "Brett was going to be the third string quarterback that season behind Don Majkowski and Mike Tomczak. He was going to sit a season and learn. Don was the starter, and Mike Tomczak made the mistake of negotiating a new contract, and he held out. That allowed Brett to get more practice time. Don was going to be our starter. He'd be in the Pro Bowl, and I thought Don Majkowski was going be a good quarterback for us. Then he got hurt."

As for the tales of Favre calling plays and formations that didn't exist, Mariucci admits some of what Favre called was a mystery, although, at least in structure, Favre wasn't that far out in left field.

Mariucci remembers Favre calling an audible for a sprint option play that went to the wrong side.

"(Holmgren) yells at me in the headset, 'What is he doing?,' and I said 'How do I know?'" Mariucci recalls. "I got ripped so bad that I didn't even need my headset to hear Mike. He was really yelling. So Brett comes off the field and I ask him what he was doing, and he said, 'It was there. I can throw that.' I said, 'We don't even practice that.' But that was Brett.

"He hadn't had a whole lot of practice before the Cincinnati game. He was running the scout team. So when Don got hurt, Mike asked me if Brett was ready. I said, 'I've got my fingers crossed.'"

And that game was a microcosm of Brett's career. He fumbled the ball; he ran around like a crazy man in the pocket. He made some big-time throws. He was lucky.

In short, he was already being the Brett Favre everyone would come to love and fear and be amazed by.

And Krumrie, the author of this amazing show, didn't know what to do.

"He was a wild horse rider," he said. "You didn't know where he was going to go. You jump on a wild horse, you don't know where he's going to go, either. And if *he* doesn't know where he's going, *you* certainly don't, and you realize just how dangerous those guys are. He overcame a lot of things on the football field."

The story is now legendary in Green Bay.

Trailing, 23-17, with barely a minute left to play, the Packers had the ball on their own 8-yard line with no timeouts remaining, needing a touchdown to win.

So that's what Favre did.

A short pass to Harry Sydney was followed by an acrobatic 44-yard reception by Sterling Sharpe to the Bengals' 44-yard line. A pass over the middle to Vince Workman resulted in a nine-yard gain to the Bengals' 35. After Favre spiked the ball to stop the clock, he pump-faked and found Kitrick Taylor streaking down the right sideline for the touchdown with thirteen seconds remaining.

So overwhelmed was Favre that he took off his helmet and ran around the field, forgetting he still had to be the holder for the extra point that would win the game.

"What a lot of people don't know is that Don Majkowski was also our holder for field goals and extra points, so Brett had to take that role," Mariucci said. "He was the back-up holder, and he only practiced it once in a while. So after he throws that touchdown pass, he was going crazy, celebrating on the sidelines, and Mike says, 'Where's the holder?' So he came out there late, and he really didn't even hold the ball. He caught it and let it go, and the ball stuck straight up."

And it stayed up long enough for Chris Jacke to kick the extra point through the uprights. And a legend was born.

Favre completed 22 of 39 passes for 289 yards and two touchdowns that day, leading Green Bay back from a 17-3 deficit.

It was the first win of Holmgren's career, the first win for Favre, and it signaled the start of a magical run that would last eighteen seasons.

"Everything happened in that game," Mariucci said. "Lucky, crazy, good, awful. And it continued for the next 321 games."

Favre started the next week against the Pittsburgh Steelers and never relinquished that starting job until 2009, when he decided to retire before changing his mind. But his heir apparent, Aaron Rodgers, had already taken over, and, faced with a nearly impossible situation on multiple fronts, the Packers dealt Favre to the New York Jets.

Favre retired again after that season but was lured back by the Minnesota Vikings, signing a free agent deal and posting one of the best seasons of his career. He nearly led the Vikings to the Super Bowl that season and retired again, only to be drawn back for one more season. But injuries and inconsistency, as well as time and age, finally caught up with him, and Favre ended that season on the bench, battered and finally ready to call it quits once and for all.

Favre ended up winning three NFL Most Valuable Player Awards, leading the Packers to two Super Bowls (one victory), and setting dozens of NFL passing records. In 2016, Favre was named to the Pro Football Hall of Fame.

And Tim Krumrie still smiles about it and knows that, very likely, none of the Favre legend would have happened were it not for a confluence of events on that warm September afternoon in 1992.

"He kicked our butts," he said. "I never would have known that, number one, I was the person who was responsible for that."

Krumrie, aside from his tackle that ushered Favre onto the field, is also known for the gruesome leg injury he had suffered four years earlier in the Super Bowl against San Francisco. His left leg, which was shattered in two places, needed a fifteen-inch titanium rod inserted, but he returned to play the next season.

He believes he and Favre share a similar history.

"He went through hell and I did, too," Krumrie points out. "But he did it for the passion of the game. We have those stories, and you can tell them forever. They ask, 'Why did you play the game?', and it's because when it's all over, it's the stories you can tell your buddies."

And his story from that September afternoon in 1992 is tops on his list.

"It's an image and identity to carry forever, and I'm sure Brett carries that around," he adds. "I still carry that story, and I think that's great."

He laughs again.

"My kids say I should be in the Hall of Fame for that."

Krumrie says he's run into Favre several times over the years, and the two still share the story of what and why and how it all happened. But, Krumrie laughs, he's still waiting Favre to thank him for providing the opening he needed to become the quarterback few NFL fans will ever forget.

As for Majkowski? His career was never the same. He left Green Bay the following season and played for the Indianapolis Colts in 1993-94 before moving on to the Detroit Lions and retiring after the 1996 season due, in large part, to that ankle injury that never really healed.

Krumrie chalked the whole incident up to the vagaries of the NFL, a fluke injury that no one could have predicted, with results that stagger the imagination.

Asked if he's seen Majkowski since that day, he laughed again.

"I haven't seen him since then," he said. "I think he'd probably hit me."

And he laughs one more time.

FACING AARON RODGERS

EVERYONE KNOWS THE story. There was the record-setting University of California quarterback Aaron Rodgers, considered by some NFL experts the best college quarterback in the 2005 NFL Draft, still sitting and waiting to be selected as the long, embarrassing day played out for a national TV audience.

Finally selected with the 24th pick in the first round by a Green Bay Packers team that wasn't sure it even needed a quarterback, Rodgers swore he would take his feelings of frustration and anger and chagrin and turn it into the fuel that would make him memorable.

Indeed, his mental fortitude again came into play in the summer of 2008 when he found himself deep in the soap opera that was the Brett Favre retirement saga that wasn't.

Favre had decided that March, after a painful January overtime playoff loss to the New York Giants, that he would retire.

"I can still play," Favre said through the tears. "I just don't know that I want to."

Stepping into the vacuum was Rodgers, who had sat for three years behind Favre waiting for his chance. But when Favre decided four months later, at the start of training camp, that he no longer wanted to retire, Rodgers was caught in the middle.

FACING THE GREEN BAY PACKERS

Favre tried to return but the Packers made it clear that he could only compete for the starting job with Rodgers but would not simply get the job back. Furious, Favre balked and, after dramatic negotiations with general manager Ted Thompson and head coach Mike McCarthy, it was decided Favre would indeed step away.

He was soon traded to the New York Jets and the quarterback job went to Rodgers, who had to deal with angry Packers fans as well as rival defenses.

Indeed, in his first preseason start, Rodgers heard boos roll through Lambeau Field as fans tried to envision life without Favre.

But Rodgers eventually won over the fans and, three years later, directed the Packers to a Super Bowl XLV win over the Pittsburgh Steelers in which he was named the game's MVP.

Now considered one of the game's best quarterbacks, he has continued the Packers incredible streak of success that comes from quality quarterback play and that other teams look on with amazement.

"It speaks to the leadership, it speaks to the Ron Wolfs and Ted Thompsons who put those teams together," said former quarterback Mark Brunell, who played for several teams including the Packers, Jacksonville Jaguars, New Orleans Saints and New York jets. "They've also been fortunate to have Brett Favre and then Aaron Rodgers. They've had quarterbacks for a long time and they're two of the best of in the business. That's the name of the game. That's where it starts."

Harry Sydney

His teams: San Francisco 49ers 1987-91; Green Bay Packers 1992

IREMEMBER WHEN I was with the 49ers and he'd come up and visit the practice facility. He was just another scrawny little kid looking to see what he could see. He was around a lot too and I learned later what a big 49ers fan he was.

I've been in Green Bay for years now and the thing you saw in Aaron Rodgers early–it was different from Brett Favre but it was the same–you saw the confidence he had in his ability and in his arm. He was always calm. It was funny because the pro game had already slowed down for him. Maybe it was because he had been sitting back for a few years and watching Brett, but his growing curve had already started. He seemed older than his years.

I remember the year (2008) when Brett retired (for the first time) and Aaron was set to take over and how awful that was. It was tough for Aaron because nobody wants to be the guy pushing out the legend and that's how he was viewed by a lot of fans. It wasn't about the Packers and Brett but that's how it was viewed and because of that, you had to pick a side. You had to pick Favre or the Packers and you had a huge split. But I think Brett brought it on himself.

And I was frustrated to see how a player was holding a team hostage. The guy driving everything (general manager Ted Thompson) has to keep the team moving and Aaron was kind of caught up in that. After (Favre's father) Irv died, Brett kind of went his own way for a while. He just didn't realize it was a case of people realizing we get old.

But Aaron came through it great and he's there. He's there, man. Because of what he's already accomplished Aaron Rodgers will always be in the room with all the tables but there are only a few sitting at the head table. Joe Montana, Tom Brady, guys who have won multiple Super Bowls.

Because the game has changed so much, I think you have to win three now to be considered one of the truly great quarterbacks. John Elway has two rings but was it because of him or because he had a great defense? Nobody really talks about Terry Bradshaw at the elite table.

You look at the Packers and to have two elite quarterbacks since 1992 and only have won two Super Bowls? That's ridiculous. It's a question of are you winning Super Bowls? You've got to win. That's what matters. And Aaron is among the best but he needs at least one more Super Bowl to really take his place among the greatest. But he can do that. He's right there.